W9-BBE-531

WITHDRAWN
FROM
COLLECTION

FORDHAM
UNIVERSITY
LIBRARIES

Logical Positivism

Edited by the author

Essential Readings in Logical Positivism
Fundamental Problems in Philosophy

LOGICAL POSITIVISM

Oswald Hanfling

Columbia University Press · New York
1981

© Oswald Hanfling 1981

All rights reserved

Published in 1981 in the
United States of America
by Columbia University Press

Library of Congress Cataloging in Publication Data

Hanfling, Oswald.
  Logical positivism.

  Includes bibliographical references.
  1. Logical positivism.   I. Title.
B824.6.H26   146'.42   81–6175
ISBN 0–231–05386–X   AACR2

Fordham University
LIBRARY
AT
LINCOLN CENTER
New York, N. Y.

Printed in Great Britain

CONTENTS

ACKNOWLEDGEMENT

I am grateful to Godfrey Vesey and Peter Winch for their help and encouragement in the course of this work.

ABBREVIATIONS

(Full publication details are given in the Bibliography.)

EL   = C. L. Stevenson, *Ethics and Language.*
ER   = O. Hanfling (ed.) *Essential Readings in Logical Positivism.*
FEK = A. J. Ayer, *The Foundations of Empirical Knowledge.*
GA   = Moritz Schlick, *Gesammelte Aufsätze.*
LP   = A. J. Ayer (ed.), *Logical Positivism.*
LSL   = Rudolf Carnap, *The Logical Syntax of Language.*
LTL   = A. J. Ayer, *Language, Truth and Logic.*
PB   = Ludwig Wittgenstein, *Philosophische Bemerkungen.*
PE   = Moritz Schlick, *Problems of Ethics.*
PI   = Ludwig Wittgenstein, *Philosophical Investigations.* (References are to section numbers in part I of the work, unless otherwise stated.)
PLP = Friedrich Waismann, *The Principles of Linguistic Philosophy.*
PP   = Moritz Schlick, *Philosophical Papers,* volume II.
TM   = Rudolf Carnap, 'Testability and Meaning', reprinted in H. Feigl and M. Brodbeck (eds.), *Readings in the Philosophy of Science.*
US   = Rudolf Carnap, *The Unity of Science.*
WWK = Friedrich Waismann, *Ludwig Wittgenstein und der Wiener Kreis.* (I have sometimes made use of the recently published translation, *Ludwig Wittgenstein and the Vienna Circle.*)

1 Introduction

'Logical positivism', we are told in the *Encyclopedia of Philosophy,* 'is dead, or as dead as a philosophical movement ever becomes'.[1] It is safe to say that few philosophers nowadays would be willing to describe themselves as Logical Positivists or Logical Empiricists. As long ago as 1956, a defender of that view acknowledged its current standing by the use of asterisks.[2] Another philosopher, writing in 1963, remarked that to discuss the 'verifiability theory of meaning' might be 'flogging a dead horse', because, he said, 'there are no longer any logical positivists left'.[3] A leading advocate of the doctrine, asked in 1979 what he now saw as its main defects, replied: 'I suppose the most important . . . was that nearly all of it was false.'[4]

Nevertheless Logical Positivism has left a mark on Philosophy that is still very much in evidence today. There is still an overall concern about meaning and a desire to produce a 'theory of meaning'. There is still a widespread belief in the 'unity of science' — the view that all descriptions, whether of animate or inanimate things, can be reduced to the vocabulary of physics. And even if the 'verifiability theory' is not accepted, it is still regarded as one of the standard options, and a standard point of departure, in discussions of meaning and in philosophy generally. A student of philosophy today

---

[1] John Passmore, in *The Encyclopedia of Philosophy,* ed. Paul Edwards (1972), under 'Logical Positivism'. This term is usually regarded as equivalent to 'Logical Empiricism'. See my remarks below.

[2] David Rynin, 'Vindication of L*G*C*L P*S*T*V*SM', in *Proceedings and Addresses of the American Philosophical Association* (1957). It should be said that Rynin was giving his Presidential address and used the occasion to display his wit. Rynin's able defence of Logical Positivism will be discussed in section 3.2.

[3] He went on to discuss it nevertheless. J. O. Wisdom in *Mind* (1963), p. 335. Verifiability, as we shall see, was one of the main concerns of the Logical Positivists.

[4] A. J. Ayer in an interview with Brian Magee. See B. Magee (ed.), *Men of Ideas* (BBC, 1978), p. 131. He went on, however, to agree that he still believed in 'the same general approach'.

could hardly fail to encounter it, and he will be expected to know what may be said for and against it.

Logical Positivism has also left its mark on the wider public. This has come about especially through A. J. Ayer's exposition of it in *Language, Truth and Logic,* a work which first appeared in 1936 and is still widely read today. This book has affected the ideas of many ordinary readers concerning philosophical, ethical and religious questions; and many think that it is typical of the philosophizing of our time.

Logical Positivism was a revolutionary movement which originated in the 1920s among the philosophers of the 'Vienna Circle'. The following is a typical quotation from their writings. 'Can it be that so many men, of various times and nations, outstanding minds among them, have devoted so much effort, and indeed fervour, to metaphysics, when this consists in nothing more than words strung together without sense?' The question was put by Rudolf Carnap, a leading member of the Circle, in an essay called 'The Elimination of Metaphysics through Logical Analysis of Language'.[5] The members of the Circle saw themselves as occupying a special place in the history of philosophy. This history, dating from the earliest times, had come, they thought, to a decisive turning point. The greater part of it, metaphysics, was to be written off as nonsense. The term 'nonsense' was used here, not merely to express strong disagreement or disapproval, but as an exact description of metaphysical statements, something that followed from a 'logical analysis of language'. It was thought that all genuine questions must be capable of scientific treatment, and all genuine knowledge part of a single system of science.

The Vienna Circle began as a group of like-minded philosophers and scientists under the leadership of Moritz Schlick,

---

[5] 'Überwindung der Metaphysik durch logische Analyse der Sprache', *Erkenntnis,* vol. II (1931). 'Overcoming' or 'conquest' of metaphysics might be a better translation. I have used the title of the translation published in A. J. Ayer's collection, *Logical Positivism.*

professor of philosophy at the University of Vienna. After some years of regular discussion meetings, the Circle organized its first international congress in 1929, attracting sympathizers from many countries, including Britain, Germany and Scandinavia. In 1930 it took over a journal, renamed *Erkenntnis,* for the publication of its ideas. The British philosopher A. J. Ayer attended the meetings of the Circle in 1933 and made its ideas widely known in the English-speaking world with the publication of *Language, Truth and Logic.*

By that time the dispersal of the Circle was already under way. Some members had taken up appointments elsewhere; Schlick, a man loved and admired by those who knew him, was shot by an insane student in 1936; and as the decade went on, political circumstances caused the emigration of members and sympathizers from Vienna, Berlin and elsewhere, mainly to the United States and Britain. To some extent the work of the Circle was carried on, for example by Carnap and Herbert Feigl in the United States; but of course there were developments and changes, and in any case the original cohesion of the Circle was lost.

One member of the Circle, Otto Neurath, was a Marxist, and saw its work, together with the advance of radical socialism, as part of a general movement towards a more enlightened and 'scientific' future. But Neurath was an exception. Political questions did not normally enter into the deliberations or writings of the Circle. They did see themselves as revolutionaries, but what they sought to overturn was a traditional conception of philosophy and science, and not the existing order of society.

The disintegration of the Circle was not only due to physical causes; there were also intellectual differences. A reader of the works of Schlick and Carnap, for example, will soon be struck by a difference of style; and this is symptomatic of a difference in philosophical outlook, one that may in the end be judged more important than what these leading members of the Circle had in common. The difference became more marked after the contact with Ludwig Wittgenstein in 1927 and especially from 1929. From this date Wittgenstein declined to meet with Carnap and other members of the Circle, but continued regular meetings with Schlick and Friedrich Waismann.

Wittgenstein's *Tractatus Logico-Philosophicus,* though written some years before the inception of the Circle, had been regarded by its members as a classic statement of the new outlook in philosophy. The work was read out and discussed sentence by sentence at the Circle's regular meetings in 1924–25 and 1925–26.[6] But Wittgenstein himself, far from being in on these developments, had altogether retired from philosophy after the publication of his book. It was largely due to Schlick that he was coaxed out of this retirement. They first met in 1927; and in 1929 there began the conversations with Schlick and Waismann, which the latter recorded in shorthand and which have since been published.[7]

Although Wittgenstein never became a member of the Vienna Circle, it was he, apparently, who first formulated the principle by which the new philosophy became known — the verification principle, according to which 'the meaning of a proposition is the method of its verification'.[8] His influence on Schlick and Waismann was very great, and in Schlick's expositions of the new philosophy there are frequent acknowledgments to Wittgenstein. The relation with Waismann was especially remarkable.[9] Under the encouragement of Schlick, Waismann took on the task of recording Wittgenstein's latest ideas and communicating them to others. To this end

---

[6] 'Neurath made frequent interjections, "metaphysics!", during the Circle's reading and discussion of Wittgenstein's *Tractatus,* to the irritation of Moritz Schlick who finally told him he was interrupting the proceedings too much. Hans Hahn, as conciliator, suggested to Neurath just to say "M" instead. After much humming — so C. G. Hempel was later told — Neurath made another suggestion to Schlick: "I think it will save time and trouble if I say 'non-M' every time the group is *not* talking metaphysics"' (editors' note in M. Neurath and R. S. Cohen, eds., *Otto Neurath: Empiricism and Sociology,* pp. 82–3). Neurath's view will be discussed in section 5.2.

[7] Friedrich Waismann, *Wittgenstein und der Wiener Kreis.*

[8] See Carnap's note of 1957 in A. J. Ayer, *Logical Positivism,* p. 146; also Carnap's autobiography in P. Schilpp (ed.), *The Philosophy of Rudolf Carnap,* pp. 45 and 57.

[9] The following details are taken from Gordon Baker's 'Verehrung und Verkehrung: Waismann and Wittgenstein', in C. G. Luckhardt (ed.), *Wittgenstein: Sources and Perspectives* (Cornell UP, 1979), pp. 243–285.

he wrote a number of papers, including 'Logische Analyse des Wahrscheinlichkeitsbegriffs' (published in the first volume of *Erkenntnis,* 1930–31), in which the verification principle was published for the first time. He also gave verbal reports of Wittgenstein's ideas, as expressed in conversations, at the regular meetings of the Circle. In addition, there was a long-term understanding whereby Waismann would put Wittgenstein's ideas into systematic form for publication in a book. This book was advertised in the first volume of *Erkenntnis,* but after various difficulties and tensions Wittgenstein withdrew from the project in 1935. Waismann continued to revise the manuscript, but it was not published in his lifetime. The much revised version finally appeared in English in 1965, under the title *Principles of Linguistic Philosophy.*

An earlier product of the collaboration had been the short 'Thesen', written down by Waismann about 1930, and published (in 1967) in the volume *Wittgenstein und der Wiener Kreis.* This work is a sort of verificationist version of the *Tractatus,* in which, for example, the verification principle is juxtaposed with propositions taken from the *Tractatus.* (The passage in question will be quoted later.) The *Principles of Linguistic Philosophy,* on the other hand, is meant to represent Wittgenstein's ideas as they developed after his brief adherence to the verification principle, and has a good deal in common with his 'later' philosphy, as expounded in the *Blue and Brown Books* and the *Philosophical Grammar.*

In some respects Wittgenstein's views were at odds with those of the Circle from the beginning. 'The Wittgenstein period', wrote Neurath in a letter to Waismann in 1939, 'took you (and to some extent Schlick as well) away from our common task'.[10] Wittgenstein did not share the Circle's enthusiasm for the 'unity of science'. Nor was he happy about the confident and aggressive tone of some of their writings. This is shown by his comment on the Circle's 'manifesto' of 1929,

[10]Quoted by Gordon Baker, op. cit. For accounts of Wittgenstein's relations with the Vienna Circle, see this paper and the introduction by B. F. McGuinness to *WWK.* A short account of Schlick's life and philosophical work was contributed by Waismann to Schlick's *Gesammelte Aufsatze.* For other historical accounts see A. J. Ayer's introduction to his *Logical Positivism,* and his autobiography, *Part of my Life.* Also see Carnap's autobiography in P. A. Schilpp (ed.), *The Philosophy of Rudolf Carnap.*

entitled 'The Scientific Conception of the World: The Vienna Circle'. This paper, written by Neurath with assistance from other members, was specially bound and presented to Schlick as a mark of appreciation. Wittgenstein described the paper as 'grandiloquent' and thought that Schlick deserved something better. He added: ' "Rejection of metaphysics"! As if *that* were something new. What the Vienna School has achieved, it ought to *show* and not *say* . . .' (*WWK* p. 18).

The Vienna Circle's philosophy became known as Logical Positivism or Logical Empiricism. 'Positivism' was a term used by the nineteenth-century philosopher Auguste Comte for the view that all knowledge is derived from observable phenomena; and it came down to the Vienna Circle through Ernst Mach. The latter, who became professor of the philosophy of science at Vienna in 1895, was regarded as a sort of founding father by the Circle, which at one time called itself the 'Ernst Mach Society'. The word 'logical' may be taken to indicate the Circle's reliance on logic or its special concern with language. Some, including Schlick, have preferred 'Logical Empiricism'. This has the advantage of indicating the Circle's affinity, widely recognized, with the empiricist tradition begun by John Locke in the seventeenth century and later represented by such thinkers as J. S. Mill and Bertrand Russell. My own preference is for 'Logical Empiricism'; but, since the other name has become more current, it has been used for the title of this book.

A fundamental question in philosophy has been 'How do I know?' It could be said that modern philosophy began with a disagreement about this question in the seventeenth century. Empiricists, such as Locke, maintained that all our knowledge comes from 'sensation' — something that happens to us when we use our eyes, ears, noses and so on. They were reacting against the views of Descartes and others, who held that certain parts or aspects of knowledge are 'innate' — that we have them, or can have them, without the use of the senses. Empiricists have tried to show how all knowledge, however various, can be analysed into items of sensation. The argument (or assumption) has been that it can all be accounted for in this way, and that whatever cannot be thus accounted for, cannot be knowledge.

Logical Empiricism belongs to this tradition. It brought to it, however, a distinctive concern about meaning. The question 'How do I know that p?' now became secondary to another, namely: 'What does "p" mean?' These questions are obviously connected. To ask myself how I know that p, I must understand what 'p' means. On the other hand, an important aspect of understanding what 'p' means is understanding it what way, if any, I could come to know that p. The verification principle states the latter connection more strongly; what it says is that the meaning of 'p' is *nothing else* than the way in which one would come to know that p. 'The meaning of a proposition is the method of its verification.' So ran the principle as stated by Wittgenstein, Schlick and others. How would one verify that the postman is at the door? By looking, listening, etc.? Very well. The meaning of that proposition consists in nothing else than these methods of verifying it — or, perhaps, in what happens when these methods are employed. (The question of what exactly was meant will be discussed in due course.) It now became the task of the new empiricism to show how all meaningful statements could be analysed into suitable verification-components; whatever could not be so analysed, must be without meaning. And verification (as we shall see later) was conceived largely in empiricist terms.

The new approach may be illustrated by reference to the problem of 'other minds'. How can I know that when another person says he is in pain, he feels the same as I do when I am in pain? Can I even know that he feels anything? More generally, how can I know that other people have thoughts and feelings, when all I can observe is their bodily movements and the sounds coming from their mouths? Might I not be, for all I know, the only one who has thoughts and feelings? Such, in brief, is the problem of other minds, stated as a problem of knowledge and doubt. But in the new philosophy the problem was transformed into a question of meaning. What does it mean to say that another person has the same feeling as I have? I can verify that he has it only by observing his behaviour and the sounds coming from his mouth. Now in saying this I have, on the verificationist view, given the meaning of the statement. But then there cannot be a further problem about how one might know it to be true; for the answer to this — the method of verification — has been given in giving the very meaning of the statement. Any further question as to a feeling distinct from the observations by which the statement is verified will be meaningless. 'It is not false, be it noted, but meaningless: we have no idea at all what it is supposed to signify.'[11] Thus a question about knowledge is absorbed into a question about meaning. If the verificationist account of meaning is correct, then there is simply no such question as the traditional one about other minds. It is, on that view, a 'pseudo-question'; a typical example of the corrupt use of language by 'metaphysicians'.

The word 'metaphysics' has been used with various meanings since the time of Aristotle. What did the Logical Empiricists mean by it? To some extent the answer can be given negatively by reference to the verification principle: metaphysical statements are essentially unverifiable. They are so, not merely for technical reasons, such as the lack of a sufficiently powerful telescope, but 'in principle'. (This distinction will be further discussed in section 4.7.) Thus the other man's feeling, conceived as something distinct from observable behaviour, is (on this view) in principle unverifiable, for to verify it would require seeing 'into another person's mind' — an idea which is ruled out for other than merely technical reasons.

But, of course, not every unverifiable statement is metaphysical. In the nonsense rhymes of Edward Lear there are many statements which one would not know how to verify; but that does not make them metaphysical. Something needs to be said about the content and purport of metaphysical statements in addition to the negative point about verification. Unlike the writer of nonsense poems, the metaphysician purports to be saying something that is both meaningful and of great importance. He is talking about 'ultimate realities' — about how things really are, in some sense going beyond the reach of ordinary observation and science. It is because his statements appear to be meaningful and important that the

[11] Schlick, 'Positivism and Realism', *ER*, p. 95, *PP* p. 270.

verificationist challenge is itself important. A convenient example, this time drawn from theology, is the statement that God exists. This is usually intended, in Western religions at least, in a sense that is beyond empirical verification. There is no seeing, hearing or touching of the Being that is meant here. The verificationist treatment of this and other metaphysical statements will be considered in a later section.

The Logical Empiricists recognized two, and only two, kinds of meaningful statements. There are, firstly, empirical statements, verifiable by observation. These are the main repository of human knowledge. Secondly, there is a kind of statement, sometimes called 'analytic', where truth or falsity can be ascertained by merely reflecting on the meanings of the relevant words. Such, for example, is the statement that a postman delivers letters. Unlike 'The postman is at the door', this requires no empirical observation for its verification, but merely a knowledge of the meanings of the words. It was thought that mathematical statements could also be treated as belonging to the 'analytic' class. By contrast, the discourse of metaphysics and theology was said to consist, for the most part, of statements that could not be fitted into either class. They were, therefore, meaningless.

Now there is an eloquent expression of this view at the end of David Hume's *Enquiry Concerning Human Understanding,* published in 1748.

> When we run over libraries, persuaded of these principles, what havoc must we make? If we take in our hand any volume; of divinity or school metaphysics, for instance; let us ask, *Does it contain any abstract reasoning concerning quantity or number?* No. *Does it contain any experimental reasoning concerning matter of fact and existence?* No. Commit it then to the flames: for it can contain nothing but sophistry and illusion.

Thus were some of the main ideas of the Vienna Circle summarized nearly two centuries before its time. There is the same division of all genuine discourse into two kinds, one of them being empirical ('experimental'). Those who think of metaphysics and theology as a third kind of discourse,

become purveyors of sophistry and illusion — or as the
Logical Empiricists would put it, of pseudo-statements dres-
sed up as meaningful discourse. The tone of the passage, too,
is exactly suited to the spirit in which the Logical Empiricists set about their task. Finally, although, as I have said, the
new empiricists placed a special emphasis on their account of
meaning, this account also had its counterpart in the works
of Hume and Locke. According to them, a word has meaning
by standing for a corresponding 'idea', these ideas being produced in the mind in the course of sense-experience; and
words not referable to such ideas are meaningless.

Nevertheless there was a major difference between the new
empiricism and the old. It was a difference between logic and
psychology. In the works of the old empiricists we find psychological theories of the acquisition of ideas. We are told of
transactions between the environment, the senses and the
mind; and of operations of the mind on the data of sense-
experience. Here, for example, is a passage in which Hume
explains how we may acquire ideas of things not, apparently,
within our experience.

> When we think of a golden mountain, we only join two
> consistent ideas, *gold,* and *mountain,* with which we were
> formerly acquainted. A virtuous horse we can conceive;
> because, from our own feeling, we can conceive virtue; and
> this we may unite to the figure and shape of a horse, which
> is an animal familiar to us.[12]

Here we have a description of mental processes, showing
how the ideas in question can be composed out of ideas of
experience. But such an account would not have interested
the Logical Empiricists. What goes on in a person's mind
when he conceives, or tries to conceive, a virtuous horse or
anything else, would be, on their view, of no philosophical
interest. What was required to understand the idea in question was to examine its logical relations. It would be relevant
to say, for example, that the statement 'This is a virtuous

---

[12] *Enquiry,* ed. Selby-Bigge, p. 19.

horse' is a *truth-function* of 'This is a horse' and 'This is virtuous'; i.e. that the truth or falsity of the first statement is dependent on the truth or falsity of the two latter statements by a strict logical relation. This may seem a trivial example, but it is only the beginning of a process of logical analysis. We should be able to break down 'This is virtuous' and 'This is a horse' into more primitive truth-functional components, and so on; ultimately arriving at basic statements which cannot be further analysed. In this way it would be made clear what the meaning of the original statement is, and what is involved in knowing or believing it.

Such, in outline, was the view of language which the Logical Empiricists took over from Wittgenstein's *Tractatus*. In this work truth-functional analysis was seen as the key to an understanding of the propositions of language. They must all be analysable into 'elementary' proposition by means of truth-functional relations. These included conjunction (*p* and *q*), disjunction (*p* or *q*), implication (*p* implies *q*) and negation (not-*p*).[13]

There was, however, a difference between the *Tractatus* and the verificationists, about the nature of the propositions coming at the end of the analysis. According to the latter, these would be statements corresponding to acts of verification (sometimes called 'observation-statements'). It was in this way that 'method of verification' was thought of as constituting the meaning both of the basic statements and of those derived from them by truth-functional relations. But this was not how the 'elementary propositions' of the *Tractatus* were conceived. They were defined by their logical properties and not by any connection with verification. An essential property of the elementary propositions of the *Tractatus* was that each is logically independent of every other. (For example, if 'This is green' entails the falsity of 'This is red', then they cannot both be elementary.) A difficulty about the *Tractatus* is whether there can be any propositions satisfying this condition. It does not seem as if observation-statements, in any ordinary sense, could do so.

[13] See, e.g., Carnap's paper 'Die alte und die neue Logik', *Erkenntnis* 1930–31.

The philosophers of the Vienna Circle, however, were inclined to read the *Tractatus* in a verificationist sense; but in
this they were carried away by their enthusiasm — both for
the *Tractatus* and for the new verificationist ideas.

There were, nevertheless, important affinities between the
Tractatus and Logical Empiricism. One of these, connected
with the role of logic, was the emphasis on statements (or
propositions)[14] as opposed to words. Philosophers like Locke
and Hume had seen the relation between a word and its
corresponding idea as the basis of meaningful language. But
the *Tractatus*, following Frege, had maintained that a word
only has meaning in the context of a proposition.[15] The
truth-functional relation, as we have seen, is a relation
between propositions. And the distinctive idea of the new
empiricism — verification — also applies to propositions
rather than words; for it makes no sense to speak of verifying
a word. Whether a word has meaning, and what meaning it
has, these can be seen as questions about the occurrence and
role of the word in meaningful statements.[16]

Another affinity between the *Tractatus* and the new
empiricism can be brought out by contrasting them with
Wittgenstein's later philosophy. In both of the former, it was
thought that the exclusion of metaphysics would be brought
about by providing a single criterion or model of language.
According to the *Tractatus*, there must be a 'general form' of
propositions. In the work of the Logical Empiricists, especially Carnap, the belief in the basic uniformity of language
emerged as a thesis about the 'unity of science' — the reducibility of all statements to a single type. But in Wittgenstein's
later philosophy, one of the main concerns was the rejection
of these ideas. Here he insisted on the diversity of language-
uses and regarded the attempt to reduce them to a single
model as misguided.[17]

[14] The choice between 'statement' and 'proposition' will be discussed in section
2.1.

[15] See especially *Tractatus* 3.3 and G. Frege, *Foundation of Arithmetic*, trans.
J. L. Austin, p. 71.

[16] See, for example, the treatment of words in Carnap's 'Elimination of Metaphysics' op. cit.

[17] See, for example, his allusion to *Tractatus* 4.5 in section 65 of the *Philosophical
Investigations*.

Three main strands may be distinguished in the thought of the Logical Empiricists: the verification principle, the elimination of metaphysics and the unity of science. The first is a statement of what meaning – the kind of meaning that language has – is. This will be discussed in chapter 2.

From the verification principle there follows a criterion of meaningfulness. If a statement has no method of verification – if it is unverifiable – then it has, according to the principle, no meaning. It was maintained that the statements of metaphysics and theology – unlike those of science and common sense – were, by this criterion, without meaning. It proved difficult, however, to formulate the criterion of verifiability in such a way as to include what was wanted and exclude what was unwanted. These difficulties are discussed in chapter 3.

Supposing that these difficulties can be overcome and that the criterion is accepted, what are the consequences for philosophy? To what extent are the statements of philosophy and religion suitable targets for elimination as intended by the criterion? And what is the status of the criterion itself? These questions will be left until chapter 7. The final chapter, chapter 8, is about the impact of the criterion on moral discourse.

The idea of the unity of science was based on the belief in the uniformity of language, and this in turn on the view that there must be a single type of act of verification and a single type of verification-statement corresponding to it. But is language analysable or reducible in this way? Two approaches to this problem, an earlier and a later, will be discussed in chapters 4 and 6. Chapter 5 will be devoted to a connected problem, that of 'privacy'. Verification, it seems, must consist of the observations of individuals. But in that case, will not the meaning of statements be private to each individual? This problem led to a major dispute among the Logical Empiricists, as will be seen.

This book is mainly about Logical Empiricism in its heyday in the twenties and thirties, and as expounded by a few leading members of the Vienna Circle. Of course there were important contributions by other members and by sympathizers in other countries. Nor did the new philosophy come to a stop after the period in question. There was, for example, a strong continuity in the many subsequent writings of Carnap. This is also evident in his contributions to the Schilpp volume of 1963. The same volume gives evidence, in the form of twenty-six 'descriptive and critical essays' by leading philosophers of the day, of the continuing interest in the kind of issues discussed by Carnap and his colleagues of the Vienna Circle. It also confirms the importance of the Circle's ideas in influencing the outlook of many leading philosophers today, in one way or another. A notable example is W. V. Quine, who actually attended at the Circle for a time. It would be interesting to trace the relations of his ideas to those of members of the Circle, but this task will not be undertaken here.

Wittgenstein's 'later' thought, starting shortly after his association with the Circle and resulting in the publication of the *Philosophical Investigations* in 1953, was another major development — though here the relation is one of rejection rather than continuity.

From time to time these and other developments will be brought into my discussions. But to deal with them comprehensively would be beyond the scope of this book — and probably any other single book. It may be hoped, however, that a discussion of some of the 'classic' writings of Logical Empiricism will be both interesting in itself and useful for its wide relevance to continuing philosophical concerns.

2 The Verification Principle

2.1 PROPOSITION, SENTENCE, STATEMENT

'The meaning of a proposition is the method of its verification.'[1] Three questions arise about this principle: What is meant by a proposition? What is meant by 'method of verification'? And (turning to the 'is') what is meant in identifying meaning with a method? These questions will occupy us in the following sections.

In the original German the word used for 'proposition' is 'Satz'; and the straightforward translation of this is 'sentence'. It is no accident, however, that the word 'sentence' was avoided. There is a difficulty about regarding sentences as true or false and, therefore, as being or not being verifiable. Such sentences as 'It is raining', 'There is a book on the table' and 'I am going out' cannot be regarded as true or false in the abstract. One cannot ask whether the *sentence* 'It is raining' is true or false; for the same sentence may be used to say something true on one occasion and something false on another; true for one speaker and false for another; true in one place and false in another. Hence it makes no sense to speak of 'the method of verification' of a sentence.[2]

It was partly in answer to such difficulties that the term 'proposition' had been introduced by philosophers. According to their usage of this word, the sentence 'It is raining', uttered on Sunday, would *express the same proposition* as 'It was raining on Sunday', uttered on Monday or Tuesday;

---

[1] For Wittgenstein's statement of the verification principle, see *WWK* pp. 227 and 244 (the latter in Waismann's 'Thesen' – see *ER* p. 27). The most frequent statements of the principle occur, however, in the writings of Schlick.

[2] Not for these sentences, anyway; it might be argued that the case is different with, e.g., the sentences of arithmetic.

15

and 'I am going out', said by me, the same proposition as 'He is going out', said by another person about me; and so on. 'Proposition' was intended as the name of that which remains true or false (as the case may be) throughout the variety of sentences, sentence-users and occasions of use.

It has been a matter of dispute among philosophers whether, and in what sense, there are such things as propositions. But if the verification principle can be formulated in terms of propositions, then the difficulty about verifying sentences will be avoided. For propositions, unlike sentences, are describable as true or false. This is so by definition.

But if the use of 'proposition' in the verification principle eliminates one problem, it creates another. This has to do with the use of the principle as a criterion of what is meaningful. A main aim of verificationism was to provide such a criterion. A proposition that had *no* method of verification would be declared to have no meaning. But it makes no sense to apply such a criterion to propositions. For a proposition, as we have seen, is by definition true or false; and something that is true or false cannot be meaningless. If the verification principle is about propositions, then it cannot serve to distinguish the meaningful from the meaningless; for it is about items which are, necessarily, meaningful. Thus the verificationist faces a dilemma. His criterion is either about propositions, and then the question 'Is it meaningful?' cannot be asked; or it is about sentences, and then the question 'Is it true?' cannot be asked. The criterion is therefore either redundant or inapplicable.[3]

What the verificationist needs in order to formulate his thesis is some item about which both questions can be asked. Now we can, in ordinary English, ask of one and the same item, a statement made by someone on a particular occasion, both whether it means anything and (if so) whether it is true.[4] Admittedly some philosophers have also defined

---

[3]This kind of objection was made by M. Lazerowitz in 'The Principle of Verifiability', *Mind* (1937), and by J. A. Passmore in 'Logical Positivism (I)', *Australasian Journal of Psychology and Philosophy* (1943) (see especially p. 70).

[4]'Statement' was the term to which Ayer resorted in his attempt to solve the problem, in the new preface to the 1946 edition of *LTL*. But in other respects my approach differs from his.

'statement' to mean something that is necessarily true or false, and hence meaningful, but the verificationist is not obliged to follow this usage. He may, following an ordinary usage, regard the expression 'meaningless statement' as a coherent one. It is true that in doing so he would forego the clearest criterion, namely the property of being true or false, for distinguishing statements (and propositions) from other uses of language. A question or a request, for example, does not have this property; nor does a word or phrase. But there are other ways of making the distinction, even if they are less clear cut and less easy to state. There are certainly utterances which appear to be statements, whether or not they are found meaningful. 'The slithy toves did gyre and gimble,' uttered by me here and now could properly be described as a meaningless statement; and this would be different from describing it as a meaningless question or a meaningless word. This view of the matter is reflected in the positivists' use of 'pseudo-statement' (or 'pseudo-proposition') to describe the utterances to which their criticism was directed. Here they assumed that there are ways of distinguishing both statements and pseudo-statements from other uses of language.

Thus the verification principle could be taken to be about the meaning and truth of particular utterances, referred to as 'statements'. But what happens, in that case, to the meaning of sentences? How is it related to the meaning of statements? The principle could be formulated so as to take account of sentences as well as statements. What it could say is that the meaning of a sentence is the method of verification of what can be stated by means of it. This would be in line with Schlick's treatment in his 'Meaning and Verification' (though he adheres to the word 'proposition').

Whenever we ask about a sentence, 'What does it mean?', what we expect is instruction as to the circumstances in which the sentence is to be used; we want a description of the conditions under which the sentence will form a *true* proposition, and of those which will make it *false*.[5]

---

[5] 'Meaning and Verification', *Philosophical Review* (1936), *GA* p. 340; *PP* p. 457.

In my discussions I shall talk as far as possible about 'statements', in the sense explained. Sometimes, however, it will be convenient to use 'proposition' or 'sentence', following the terminology of the texts quoted.

2.2 THE LEAP OUT OF LANGUAGE

The verification principle is a statement of what meaning is: it identifies meaning with a method. How are we to understand this identification? (This was the third of my questions on page 15. The second, about 'method of verification', will be dealt with in section 2.3.)

'Meaning' and 'method' are concepts of different types. A method is a way of doing something; a meaning is not. A method may or may not be carried out, it may be easy or difficult to practice, it may take such and such a time. But these things cannot be said about the meaning of a statement.

The verification principle cannot be understood in the same way as ordinary statements of meaning, as when we give the meaning of a word or sentence by means of another. If we say that the meaning of 'Il pleut' is 'It is raining', then we are saying that these sentences have the *same* meaning. But if we say that the meaning of 'Il pleut' is the method of its verification, we are not speaking of two items having the same meaning. For a method of verification cannot be said to have a meaning, at least not in the sense in which words and sentences have meaning.

How are we to understand the verification principle? Let us assume that the method of verification of 'Il pleut' is to put one's hand out of the window. Obviously 'Il pleut' does not mean 'to put one's hand out of the window'. But this is not the sort of equation that the verification principle is trying to make. It is not saying that the meaning of a statement is the same as that of another set of words — those describing a method of verification; it is, rather, identifying the meaning with the method of verification itself. Thus the sentence 'The meaning of "Il pleut" is . . .' would need, somehow, to be completed by something non-linguistic: a method of verification.

This awkwardness should not, however, be regarded as an unforeseen corollary of the principle, due perhaps to a carelessness in its formulation. On the contrary, it was thought essential to make a connection between language and something other than language. This was what Wittgenstein had attempted in the *Tractatus*. There, taking 'names' as fundamental elements of language, he had written: 'A name means an object. The object is its meaning' (3.203). Now if one wanted to state the meaning of a particular name in accordance with this dictum, one would, again, have to complete the sentence with something non-linguistic, namely the object that 'is' its meaning.[6]

When, subsequently, he came to advocate the verification principle, Wittgenstein stressed that the method of verification is not merely 'the means of establishing the truth of a proposition, it is the meaning itself.'[7] More explicit statements of the need to go beyond language are to be found in the writings of Schlick.

> ... in order to arrive at the meaning of a sentence or proposition we must go beyond propositions. For we cannot hope to explain the meaning of a proposition merely by presenting another proposition ... I could always go on asking 'But what does this new proposition mean?' You see there would never be any end to this kind of inquiry, the meaning would never be clarified if there were no other way of defining it than by a series of propositions ... The discovery of the meaning of any proposition must ultimately be achieved by some act, some immediate procedure, for instance, as the showing of yellow; it cannot be given in a proposition.[8]

[6] The *Tractatus* view will be further discussed in section 7.6.

[7] *WWK* pp. 227 and 244 (*ER* p. 27). Similarly in *Philosophische Bemerkungen*, 166(4): 'The verification is not *one* token of the truth, it is *the* sense, of a proposition. (Einstein: How a magnitude is measured is what it is.)' Compare his remarks about length on p. 225 of *Philosophical Investigations*.

[8] 'The Future of Philosophy', *GA* pp. 128–30, *PP* pp. 219–20. The slight awkwardness of expression here and elsewhere in Schlick's writings is due to his use of English rather than German. Many of his papers were written for publication in English-language journals, and the important lectures on 'Form and Content' were delivered in London. The need to 'go beyond propositions' was also stated in Waismann's 'Theses', *WWK* pp. 246–8 (*ER* pp. 29–32).

Now one might have thought, in view of Schlick's adherence to the verification principle, that the 'act' or 'immediate procedure' in question must be one of verification. But here there is an important confusion in Schlick's thought. The argument just quoted is about *explanation* of meaning. But to verify a proposition is not the same thing as to explain its meaning (or have its meaning explained). A quotation from another paper will bring out the conflation of these ideas in Schlick's mind.

> Stating the meaning of a sentence amounts to stating the rules according to which the sentence is to be used, and this is the same as stating the way in which it can be verified (or falsified). The meaning of a proposition is the method of its verification. The 'grammatical' rules will consist partly of ordinary definitions, i.e., explanations of words by means of other words, partly of what are called 'ostensive' definitions . . . . The simplest form of an ostensive definition is a pointing gesture combined with the pronouncing of the word, as when we teach a child the signification of the sound 'blue' by showing a blue object . . . .[9]

It would seem that in trying to make sense of the identification of meaning with method of verification, Schlick resorted to another method — a method, not of verification, but of explanation of meaning. This was the method of 'ostensive definition'. Here he thought he had found a way of breaking out of the circle of language, of 'going beyond propositions' as required by his argument. If I teach someone the meaning of 'blue' by means of a sample, using 'a pointing gesture combined with the pronouncing of the word', then indeed my explanation of meaning is not merely a matter of words. The sample and the pointing gesture are essential to the explanation, and they are not words.

Such an act of explanation is not, however, an act of veri-

---

[9] 'Meaning and Verification', *GA* p. 340, *PP* p. 458. In Waismann's 'Theses' we are told that the ostensive act 'goes outside language and connects signs with reality' (*WWK* p. 246, *ER* p. 29).

fication. Nor is the person who receives my explanation in the position of one who verifies the statement. For to say that he verifies it is to suppose that he already knows its meaning. We could imaging someone in that position (someone who already knows the meaning) verifying my statement 'This is blue' by looking at the sample, and perhaps replying 'That's true'. But this would make no sense if he is only then learning the meaning of the statement — if the function of my utterance is to teach it to him. Perhaps, then, what Schlick should have said is that the meaning of a statement is its method of ostensive explanation, rather than its method of verification.

It remains to consider whether the resort to ostensive explanation is as decisive a break from the circle of propositions as Schlick had thought; whether it will account for the meanings of propositions in a way that 'goes beyond propositions'. This question was one of the starting points of Wittgenstein's 'later' philosophy, after his break from verificationism. In the opening pages of the *Blue Book* (dating from 1933–34) we find the same division as that made by Schlick between two sorts of definitions. 'The verbal definition, as it takes us from one verbal expression to another, in a sense gets us no further. In the ostensive definition however we seem to make a much more real step towards learning the meaning' (p. 1).[10] But in the ensuing pages Wittgenstein proceeded to show that ostensive definition cannot be taken to play the fundamental role that had been attributed to it. If verbal definition is insufficient from one point of view, ostensive definition is so from another. An ostensive definition[11] cannot be regarded as giving a complete account of the meaning of a word in the sense in which a verbal definition can.

---

[10] Ostensive definition was among the topics discussed by Schlick and Wittgenstein, and there are frequent acknowledgements to Wittgenstein in Schlick's writings. Some of the former's remarks on ostensive definition are reported in *WWK* pp. 209–10. The term 'ostensive definition', and the distinction made by means of it, had been introduced by W. E. Johnson in his *Logic* of 1921. See part I, p. 94.

[11] It is worth noting that one would not ordinarily speak of the ostensive procedure as a definition; 'teaching' or 'explanation' would be more appropriate. On this point see *PI* 6, second paragraph.

Suppose I know the meaning of word X but am completely ignorant of the meaning of word W. Then, on learning that W means X, I have learned the meaning of W. In this case my understanding of W is wholly accounted for by the definition I have been given, together with my prior knowledge of X. But this is not so with ostensive definition. If I am completely ignorant of the meaning of W, then, on learning that *this* object (being pointed to) is W, I *may* learn the meaning of that word; but I may not. For if I am completely ignorant of its meaning, I may not know which feature of the object my teacher means when he points. In the *Blue Book* (p. 2) Wittgenstein imagined someone trying to explain the word 'tove' by pointing to a pencil and saying 'This is tove'. Does he mean 'This is a pencil', 'This is round', 'This is hard' or 'This is one'? It would help, obviously, if he could *tell* the learner which feature was meant; telling him, for example, that 'tove' is a colour-word. But in doing this he would be resorting to the verbal method, thereby showing that the ostensive method was not sufficient. However, even the explanation 'This is a colour-word' would not entail success; for it would leave open a question about the range of colours meant by 'tove' — whether it means that particular shade or a range (light tove, dark tove etc.) and if so, what that range is. Again, the meaning of the act of pointing must itself be understood by the learner. He must understand that he is to attend to an object situated in a certain direction relative to the pointing finger; otherwise he may look at the wrong object; or he may think that 'tove' means the act of pointing or that it is a name given to the teacher's finger. Finally, the learner must already have a general understanding of the *uses* of words and sentences — uses of which the ostensive situation is *not* a typical example.

All this does not mean, of course, that ostensive teaching does not work. It works because normally the learner does know which feature is meant, and does understand both the uses of words and the purpose and convention of pointing. What this means, however, is that he brings to the situation an understanding of language which cannot itself be accounted for by ostensive teaching. The objection to verbal definition was that it could not account for our understanding of language; but it turns out that ostensive definition cannot account for it either.

These limitations are even more evident if we think (in accordance with the verification principle) of statements rather than words. It is doubtful whether the idea of 'pointing to a fact' (e.g. the fact that it is raining) is even intelligible; but in any case, it is obvious that such a gesture could be taken to mean all sorts of different things.

A somewhat similar difficulty arises if we return from the idea of ostensive definition to that of verification. Just as the ostensive gesture can mean more than one thing, so a given method or act of verification will be appropriate to more than one statement. This will be so, for example, with the statements 'The carpet is blue' and 'The carpet is red', where the obvious method of verification — looking at the carpet — will be common to both statements. (A different conception of verification — one where there is a closer fit with meaning — will, however, be considered in section 4.1.)

So far, then, Schlick has not succeeded in explaining how the meaning of propositions can be accounted for by a method that goes 'beyond propositions'. We have not been given a way of making sense of the identification of meaning with an act or method of acting, as stated in the verification principle.

2.3 THE VERIFICATION PRINCIPLE AS A CRITERION OF UNDERSTANDING

It is, however, possible to take the verification principle in a less literal way, and without following Schlick in his extra-linguistic excursions. If we do so, we may find a claim which is both intelligible and reasonable. It seems clear that there is some connection between meaning and verification. Let us try saying that if a person understands the meaning of a sentence, then he must know the appropriate method of verification. There are certain passages in the writings of Schlick and Waismann which would suggest such a reading of the verification principle.

What criterion have we to find out whether the meaning of
a sentence has been grasped? ... A person knows the
meaning of a proposition if he is able to indicate exactly
the circumstances under which it would be true (and distinguish them from the circumstances which would make
it false). This is the way in which Truth and Meaning are
connected (it is clear that they must be connected in some
way). (Schlick, *GA* p. 240, *PP* p. 361, *ER* p. 36.)

A connection between truth and understanding had been
stated by Wittgenstein in the *Tractatus:* 'To understand a
proposition means to know what is the case if it is true'
(4.024). This remark was taken up and given a verificationist
interpretation in Waismann's 'Theses'.

To understand a proposition means to know what is the
case if the proposition is true.
One can understand it without knowing *whether* it is true.
To become aware of the sense of a proposition one has to
get clear about the procedure for establishing its truth.
If one does not know this procedure, then one cannot
understand the proposition either . . .
*The sense of a proposition is the method of its verifica-
tion.*[12]

If the final sentence of this − i.e. the verification principle
− is taken as saying no more than the preceding remarks,
then it may be taken as a correct expression of the relations
between statements, understanding and verification. It is
correct to say that if someone understands a statement, then
he must be 'clear about the procedure for establishing its
truth'. A similar view is also expressed in Waismann's later
work, *The Principles of Linguistic Philosophy:* 'The criterion
of understanding a sentence is the knowledge of the method
of its verification.'[13]

---

[12] *WWK* p. 244 (*ER* p. 27). The omitted passage, which, admittedly, goes against
my present suggestion, will be quoted in section 6.1. For remarks on the author-
ship of Waismann's writings, see pp. 4−5.

[13] *PLP* p. 325. Also see chapters 2 and 4 of Waismann, *How I See Philosophy.*

Let us consider this version of the verification principle in more detail. Is knowing the method of verification a necessary condition of understanding a statement? Is it a sufficient condition? We must now examine the last of the questions with which we began on page 15: what is meant by 'method of verification'?

There are, for any given statement, a variety of methods of verification. Are all of them part of 'the' method of verification, knowledge of which is necessary to understanding what the statement means? The question was considered by Wittgenstein in his Cambridge lectures of 1930–33, as recorded by G. E. Moore. At that time Wittgenstein was already expressing doubts about the verification principle, describing it as 'a mere rule of thumb, because "verification" means different things'.

> ... he went on to say ... that statements in the newspapers could verify the [proposition] that Cambridge had won the boat-race, and that yet these statements 'only go a very little way towards explaining the meaning of "boat-race" ' .[14]

In later writings Wittgenstein spoke of 'symptoms' and 'criteria'. The latter, he maintained, enter into the meanings of words in a way in which the former do not. Thus we might say 'Experience teaches that there is rain when the barometer falls', but we cannot similarly regard it as a matter of experience that we have 'certain sensations of wet and cold' when there is rain; for the latter 'is founded on a definition', and not merely on empirical discovery (*PI* 354). In terms of our question, this means that knowledge about the sensations of wet and cold is a necessary condition of understanding 'There is rain', but knowledge about the falling barometer is not.

Consider, as another example, the statement 'There is a piece of metal in this suitcase'. There are methods of verifying it which are known to electronic experts but not to ordinary people. Until recently they were not known to any-

---

[14] G. E. Moore, *Philosophical Papers*, p. 266. I have substituted 'proposition' for 'hypothesis' in the first sentence.

one. If knowledge of these methods were essential to understanding the meaning of the statement, then we must conclude
that most people do not understand it, or do not understand
it fully or properly; and, what is worse, that until recently no
one understood it fully or properly; and that further inven-
tions may show that no one does so even today. Alternatively, we may be forced to the conclusion that the meaning
of a statement changes whenever a new method of verification is found. This indeed seems to follow from the verification principle as originally formulated.

But to take this view would be to ignore a distinction that
is in fact made. If I do not know the ordinary methods of
verifying that there is a piece of metal in the suitcase, then I
cannot be said to know what the statement means; but this is
not true of the electronic methods. My ignorance of them
would not put in doubt my understanding of what the statement means. If the verification principle (whether taken as a
statement of what meaning is or as a criterion of understanding the meaning) is to express our actual connection of meaning with verification, then 'the method of verification' must
be taken to refer to those methods which are essential in the
way just explained. The terminology of the 'Theses', as
quoted on page 24, could be taken so as to accommodate
this point. What was required there as a condition of understanding was that one must 'get clear about' the method of
verification. One thing that one will have to be clear about is
the distinction between essential and non-essential methods
of verification, as applied to a given statement.

This is not to say that the distinction can always be easily
made or the essential methods easily described. A point made
by Wittgenstein in his later writings was that a given feature
may be regarded 'sometimes as a symptom, sometimes as a
criterion, of a state of affairs', with a corresponding 'oscilla-
tion' of meaning (*Zettel* 438). This could be taken in a
historical sense, relative to the progress of science. But it
could also be taken as relative to the knowledge and assumptions of those taking part in a given kind of discourse. In a
discussion among electronic experts, one might not be
credited with understanding the term 'metal' unless one knew
the electronic methods of detection. Again, the ordinary

man's use of the term 'metal' may be overridden by a metal-lurgist using scientific criteria. (That this is liable to happen is also, however, part of the ordinary man's understanding of the concept.)

But these points do not eliminate the distinction between essential and non-essential methods of verification – the former, but not the latter, being necessary conditions of an ordinary person's understanding of a statement.

Let us consider our other question, concerning sufficient conditions: whether knowledge of the appropriate methods of verification is sufficient for understanding. Here we must be careful not to take 'method of verification' in an unduly narrow sense. Verificationists commonly spoke of verification as if it were purely a matter of perceiving something in one's immediate presence. But there is more than this to a method of verification. A method involves action; it is a way of doing something. And this is also true of methods of verification. To verify that there is a piece of metal in the suitcase, or a table in the next room, I must do something; and the knowledge of what I must do is part of what is required for my understanding of the statement. In some cases the action consists in doing something *to* the object that the statement is about; for example, driving a car to verify that it will do a hundred miles per hour.

There is another respect in which 'verification' must be taken in a suitably broad sense. This concerns the variety of methods of verification (corresponding to a variety of kinds of meaning). To verify that Cambridge will win the boat-race, I need to see the Cambridge boat in front of the Oxford one at such and such a time and place. But the same observation would serve to verify the statement that, merely, the Cambridge boat is in front of the Oxford one etc.; and this obviously does not mean the same as the statement about winning a race. The latter implies an institution and a set of rules, and the former does not. This difference of meaning cannot be accounted for if all verification is thought of as being of the same type. For an institution or a set of rules cannot be observed in the sense in which a boat or a colour can be observed; nor do they exist in the same sense of 'exist'. This is not to say that there is no way of verifying their existence, or of verifying who wins the boat-race; it is to say that a different kind of verification is needed in this case.

I shall not go into the complications of this and other aspects of verification. It should not surprise us that the meaning and verification of statements are complicated and of different types. This, it is true, goes against the view commonly held by Logical Positivists, that there is a single basic type of verification – a view that will be critically examined in chapters 4 and 6. But a verificationist may accept that there is a variety of meanings and methods of verification. And this would not affect the principle that to understand a statement one must be clear about the method of verification; it would, indeed, give it an extra point. This principle, moreover, would have some application even if one admitted unverifiable statements as meaningful. For it may be said that what one has to be clear about in their case is that there is *no* method of verification. Such a use of the verification principle would not be vacuous. For there is a difference, even in this case, between someone who is clear about the method of verification – i.e. that there is none; and someone who is not. The latter could not have a proper understanding of what the statement means.

But if we take verification, and being clear about verification, in a suitably broad way, does this give us a sufficient condition for the understanding of a statement? It seems clear that this cannot be so in the case of unverifiable statements, at any rate. Understanding such a statement must involve something more specific than merely the point that it is, like others of its class, unverifiable. Perhaps what we shall require here is an ability to give *reasons* for believing the statement – as distinct from methods of verification. But there are, in any case, other aspects of understanding a statement which are not covered by the verification principle. One of them concerns a connection with action. I cannot be said to understand the statement 'Your house is on fire', if, on having it addressed to me, I take no action. Again, my understanding of 'It is raining' will manifest itself in such actions as taking an umbrella, and not merely in my ability to verify the statement. Perhaps a verificationist will reply that these matters are not 'strictly' part of the meaning of a statement, in the way in which, for example, 'wet' is part of the meaning of 'It is raining'. It is true that there is a difference here; but it would be wrong to conclude that the connection with action, being of a different kind, is no connection at all, or that it is not a logical connection. For the connection is logical, in a way in which, for example, the connection with barometers is not. An ignorance of the latter does not entail that one's understanding of 'It is raining' is put into doubt; but a failure to take suitable action does entail it.

There is also another way in which understanding is connected with appropriate action, in this case the action of speaking. Schlick was confused about this matter, as the following passage shows.

> Stating the meaning of a sentence amounts to stating the rules according to which the sentence is to be used, and this is the same as stating the way in which it can be verified (or falsified).[15]

Schlick seems to think that the question of when to use a sentence is simply a question of verification — that its use is appropriate if one has verified what the sentence says. But this is nowhere near enough. Someone who, regardless of circumstances, states every half hour that the cat is on the mat, will not be credited with knowing how to use that sentence, even if he has verified that the cat is on the mat. Knowing when, and when not, to use a sentence requires, not merely a knowledge of its truth or falsity, but a more general knowledge of human interests and situations. Schlick is right in connecting the meaning of a sentence with its use; but there is more to understanding the use of a sentence than knowing its method of verification.

Perhaps the verificationist will admit that his principle is not the whole story. He may still claim that it gives a necessary, though not sufficient, condition of understanding.

---

[15] *GA* p. 340, *PP* p. 458 (previously quoted page 20). There is a similar mistake in Michael Dummett's *Frege*, pp. 296–8. I have discussed this in my paper 'Does Language need Rules?', *Philosophical Quarterly* (1980).

Alternatively, he may try to separate out those aspects of understanding for which it gives both a necessary and a sufficient condition.

3 The Criterion of Verifiability

3.1 THE VERIFICATION PRINCIPLE AND THE CRITERION OF VERIFIABILITY

The original verification principle may have seemed at first sight to be saying something simple and straightforward. But as we have seen, doubts soon arise about what exactly the meaning of a statement is to be identified with, and in what sense of identification.

Now a main aim of verificationism was to provide a criterion for distinguishing between meaningful and meaningless statements. There is a form of verificationism which corresponds more immediately to this aim, while avoiding some of the difficulties of the verification principle. This form of verificationism consists of a criterion of meaningfulness: it says that a statement is meaningful if, and only if, it can be verified.

It was this criterion which was thought to bring about a revolution in the history of philosophy. For a long time it had been noticed that in this discipline there is a curious lack of progress. The old questions keep reappearing, and old answers to them are discussed again and again. This situation has been especially noticeable, and for some intolerable, since the rise of modern science in the seventeenth century. It is since that time that science and philosophy have become clearly separated; and while science, using empirical methods, has been astonishingly successful in providing answers, philosophy, using the methods of *a priori* reflection, finds itself returning again and again to the old problems.

It is not easy to see why this should be so. If the quest of philosophy is for *a priori* truths, then, one might have thought, it should be possible to arrive at definitive conclusions in the same sort of way as in logic and mathematics. This is not to say that the solutions must be easy to come by,

31

or that all problems must have a solution. The first of these points is not true of logic and mathematics either, and the second is doubtful. But at least one would expect to find definitive solutions to a large range of problems – or rather, to find that these solutions have already been found. But this is not the case in philosophy. If, on the other hand, philosophical statements aim to go beyond the domain of *a priori* truth, then, one might have thought, they should be open to verification in the same sort of way as the empirical statements of science and of everyday conversation. But this again is not the case.

How is this state of affairs to be explained? One way of dealing with it is to say that there is something odd about the meaning of philosophical questions – or to put it more boldly, that though they look like meaningful questions, they are in fact without meaning. This might explain why these questions are as perplexing as they are. Now according to the verificationists, the very fact of being unanswerable showed a question to be meaningless. According to the criterion of verifiability, a question has meaning only if there is some way of verifying the statements that might be given in answer to it. This, it was thought, was the test that was passed by statements of science and failed by the statements of traditional philosophy. 'The scientific conception of the world,' we are told in the 1929 'manifesto', 'does not acknowledge any insoluble riddles. The clarification of traditional philosophical problems leads to the result that they are partly shown up as pseudo-problems and partly transformed into empirical problems and thus subject to the verdict of empirical science.'[1]

The idea of a statement, or other expression, which appears to be meaningful but is not really so, is familiar enough. Anyone who reads the newspapers or, let us say, certain writings of social scientists, will find himself asking, from time to time, what, if anything, a given statement means; and he may conclude that it means nothing – though he may be hard put to it to prove this or to say what it is that makes the difference between meaningful and meaningless.

---

[1] *Erkenntnis* I, p. 15. (This is the paper referred to on pp. 5–6.)

Similarly, according to the positivists, it commonly happens in philosophy that an expression which appears to have meaning is in truth meaningless. Carnap, in his 'Elimination of Metaphysics through Logical Analysis of Language', took the word 'principle' as an example. This word may be used in various contexts and with various verification-conditions. But, said Carnap, when a metaphysician speaks of 'the principle of the World' or 'the principle of Being', he does not, it appears, mean the word in accordance with any such conditions. What he says is unverifiable and therefore meaningless.[2] Waismann, in a later writing, asked the reader to imagine someone saying: 'The universe has expanded to twice its original size this night.'

How would the world appear to us on waking up in the morning? Well − just exactly as before. All things have become twice as large, consequently also the standard with which I measure, and thus I shall count with it the same number of metres . . . In short, this remarkable change of our world could not be verified in any way . . .[3]

The criterion of verifiability must not be confused with the verification principle. The latter was intended to answer such questions as 'What is meaning?' and 'What does the meaning of a statement consist in?' But the criterion of verifiability does not attempt these questions. It is (or purports to be) merely a way of deciding whether a given statement has meaning or not. The criterion is more modest than the principle; it is entailed by, but does not entail, the principle. It follows from the principle that where there is no method of verification, there is no meaning; and this is what the criterion asserts. But someone who adheres to the criterion is not thereby committed to a view about what meaning con-

---

[2] *Erkenntnis* II, pp. 154−5.

[3] *PLP* p. 326. The neatness of the example, as Waismann went on to point out, is spoilt by the fact that there would be differences in weights and densities. Interesting examples of claims that have actually been made are given on pp. 328−9.

sists in. He may indeed regard this as an improper question.[4]

The criterion of verifiability seems likely to combine an avoidance of such questions with the commonsense appeal of verificationism. A common way of finding out what someone means by a statement is to ask how we might set about verifying it. And if no answer to this were forthcoming, then we might indeed conclude that the statement is meaningless, or meaningless as far as that person is concerned. A. J. Ayer was one philosopher who advocated the criterion of verifiability without the verification principle. He wrote:

> We say that a sentence is factually significant to any person if, and only if, he knows how to verify the proposition which it purports to express — that is, if he knows what observations would lead him, under certain conditions, to accept the proposition as being true, or reject it as being false. (*LTL* p. 48.)

By means of such a criterion it was hoped to proceed immediately to the elimination of metaphysics, without getting involved in questions of what meaning consists in. But the modesty of this form of verificationism can also be seen as a drawback. In the verification principle we had a general theory of meaning, from a particular application of which the elimination of metaphysics was thought to follow. According to the theory, if the method of verification of a statement is this and this, then its meaning, likewise, is this and this. If the statement is, say, a general one, or one about the past or the future, then the method of verification, and likewise the meaning, will be of such and such a kind.[5] The theory might be applied equally well (though it was not in fact so applied)

---

[4]Compare Ayer's rejection of the 'relational theory' of meaning, in his *Foundations of Empirical Knowledge*, pp. 97–8. 'We cannot find "the other term of the relation of meaning" because the assumption that meaning is a relation which somehow unites a symbol with some other unspecified object is itself erroneous . . . There is no one thing that all symbols mean.' The relational theory is criticized by J. L. Evans in 'On Meaning and Verification', *Mind* (1953). See also A. R. White, *Mind* (1954).

[5]These and other kinds of statements, and their methods of verification, will be discussed in chapter 4.

to analytic statements and statements of mathematics. Here there are non-empirical methods of verification, corresponding to the kind of meaning that these statements have. Finally, in the case of metaphysical statements, the method of verification is (allegedly) nil; and so the meaning likewise must be nil. Here the criterion of verifiability can be seen as a consequence of a general theory. And as in science a particular law may find readier acceptance by being part of a general theory, so it may be here with the criterion of verifiability. But if the latter is propounded without the backing of a theory, then it may look like a mere *ad hoc* device to support a prejudice against certain kinds of discourse.

Now in spite of a certain commonsense appeal, the criterion of verifiability does not always seem to accord with ordinary uses of 'meaningless' and 'meaningful'. In a broadcast debate with Father F. C. Copleston, Ayer introduced the word 'drogulus'.[6] A drogulus, he said, was to be 'not the sort of thing you can see or touch, it has no physical effects of any kind, but it's a disembodied thing'. He then supposed that he had told Copleston: 'A drogulus is standing just behind you'. Ayer was unwise enough to end on a rhetorical question: 'Does that make sense?' Copleston replied that it did make sense. He did not see that the question depended on verifiability; he could, he claimed, form the idea of such a disembodied being from his ideas of body and mind, and this was enough to give it sense.

Perhaps many listeners would have agreed with Ayer that the answer to his question was, as he intended, 'no'. But others would have been doubtful or sided with Copleston. The example is, in any case, more favourable to Ayer's case than would be, say, an example drawn from actual religious discourse. For whereas 'drogulus' is an *ad hoc* introduction, having no connections with any actual discourse or practice, this could hardly be said about religious statements. In any case, someone who described his religious beliefs as unverifiable would not be taken to have described them *thereby* as meaningless.

---

[6] 'Logical Positivism – A Debate'. See Paul Edwards and Arthur Pap (eds.), *A Modern Introduction to Philosophy*, p. 747.

Supporters of the criterion of verifiability often felt a difficulty in explaining and defending their use of the word 'meaningless'. Carnap, unconsciously paraphrasing *Pickwick Papers,* placed the following 'Advice to the Reader' at the front of his monograph *The Unity of Science:*[7]

> *Nonsense* (or *pseudo*-expression) is intended to carry none of its usual abusive connotation. Technical use = whatever cannot be verified in experience. (P. 30.)[8]

Sometimes the qualification 'cognitive' was used to soften the epithet 'meaningless'. Thus it was 'cognitive meaning' that the statements under criticism were said to lack. But this use of 'cognitive' again requires explanation. Is it claimed that someone who says 'I know that my redemeer liveth' would simply be contradicting himself? Or is the word 'cognitive' also being used in a technical, Pickwickian sense?

But whatever may be said about these questions, much of the interest of verificationism, and of the verifiability criterion in particular, lay in the attempt to provide a clear way of distinguishing metaphysics from science, of bringing out the essential difference between them. Perhaps, if the distinction were made sharp enough, it might be said that the two kinds of statements were not even *statements* in the same sense; so that if we use this word in the one case, it would be better to speak in the other case of 'pseudo-statements' (though this expression, again, has its connotations). In any case, much of the effort of verificationists has been devoted to the attempt to show how their criterion could be applied so as to bring out the distinction in question.

But, as often happens with such criteria, it soon became evident that the criterion must be evaluated by reference to the data, rather than the other way round. For there arose

---

[7] 'Die Physikalische Sprache als Universalsprache der Wissenschraft', *Erkenntnis* (1932); translated by Max Black and published in a separate volume as *The Unity of Science.*

[8] In Charles Dickens' novel Mr Blotton is made to agree that when he called Mr Pickwick a humbug, he had meant this word in a special sense and not with its usual connotations.

various problems about applying the criterion so as to yield the 'right' results — in dealing with statements that were recognized, antecedently to the criterion, as examples of science or metaphysics. Some of these problems were discussed in the course of modifications to Ayer's criterion, as quoted above.

3.2 'STRONG' AND 'WEAK' VERIFICATION

The criterion quoted above will not do as it stands, because not enough is said about the relevance of the observations mentioned. All sorts of observations might conceivably 'lead [someone], under certain conditions, to accept the proposition as being true, or reject it as being false'. But it would not follow that he had *verified* the proposition. The observations need to be related to the meaning of the proposition in a closer way than merely bringing it about — causing it to come about — that one accepts the proposition as being true. An adherent of the verification principle (as distinct from the criterion of verifiability) might put the point by saying that the observation must be one that is *meant* by the proposition. But Ayer put the matter in terms of logical deduction. The test was to consist in the deducibility of 'experiential propositions' from the proposition under test.

> Let us call a proposition which records an actual or possible observation an experiential proposition. Then we may say that it is the mark of a genuine factual proposition, not that it should be equivalent to an experiential proposition, or any finite number of experiential propositions, but simply that some experiential propositions can be deduced from it in conjunction with certain other premises without being deducible from those other premises alone. (*LTL* p. 52.)

As has been pointed out, Ayer's intention was to provide merely a criterion of meaningfulness, and not a theory of meaning as in the case of the verification principle. His criterion was also 'modest' in another way, indicated by the

phrase 'but simply that some . . .'. In common with other
verificationists, Ayer held that the statements of science and
ordinary language, though certainly meaningful, were not
'completely' or 'conclusively' verifiable. In introducing the
criterion just quoted, he wrote: 'If we adopt conclusive verifiability as our criterion of significance, as some positivists
have proposed, our argument will prove too much' (*LTL*
p. 50). It would prove too much, Ayer thought, because it
would exclude, for example, general statements and statements about the past. These, he said, could never be 'conclusively verified'; 'their truth can never become more than
highly probable' (pp. 50, 51). A general statement, such as
'All men are mortal' could not be verified, it was thought,
because the statement is about an unlimited class, whereas
only a finite number of instances could be observed. It would
not be self-contradictory to suppose that the statement were
false, in spite of all the instances that had been observed.
Moreover, it soon appeared that a similar sort of scepticism
must infect ordinary particular statements about tables and
chairs. Thus 'all empirical propositions are hypotheses which
are continually subject to the test of further experience'
(p. 13).[9]

Ayer's criterion was intended to provide a way of certify-
ing suitable statements as meaningful without the need for
'conclusive' verifiability. It was enough, he said, if 'some
experiential proposition can be deduced' from the proposition under test; this would make it verifiable in what he
called a 'weak sense', and hence meaningful.

There are, however, a number of obscurities and difficulties about the criterion. In the first place, a reader may be
puzzled by the talk about 'certain other premises'. These
were required in order to make the connection between the
statement under test and the relevant observation-statements.
From the statement 'It is raining on Dartmoor' it obviously
does not follow that any relevant observations are taking
place. The claim must be, rather, that such observations
would be made *if* certain other premises were true; for

[9] These claims, as applied to various types of statements, will be discussed in
chapter 4.

example, if one happened to be on Dartmoor. Then, as Ayer says, the observation-statements would not be 'deducible from [the latter] premises alone', but only from them in conjunction with the statement under test – i.e. that it is raining on Dartmoor.

It would seem that Ayer thought of the matter in terms of strict deduction. It was because of the lack of such deduction *from* observation-statements *to* the statements to be tested that he rejected the idea of conclusive verifiability as the 'criterion of significance'. But can there be a strict deduction the other way round? In what sense are observation-statements deducible from premises of the kind I have mentioned? Here we need to enquire what Ayer had in mind when speaking of an observation-statement (or 'experiential proposition'). He seems to have regarded 'This is white' as a typical example.[10] But it is far from clear how the statement 'This is white' could be deduced from, say, the premises 'There is snow outside' and 'I am looking out of the window'. No doubt there is a logical connection here, but it is not one of deduction. (This matter will be further discussed in chapter 4.)

There are further difficulties about Ayer's idea of verification. Having introduced the contrast between strong (i.e. 'conclusive') and weak verification, he went on to claim that *no* propositions are verifiable in the strong sense. 'No proposition is capable, even in principle, of being verified conclusively' (*LTL* p. 179).

In a paper published after the book's first appearance, Morris Lazerowitz objected that if strong verification is impossible 'even in principle', then Ayer had not succeeded in giving sense to this notion; nor had he given sense to the contrast between weak and strong, in terms of which the essential 'weak sense' was supposed to be expounded.[11] Ayer responded to this in the introduction to the second edition of his book. He had now come to think, he said, that 'there is a class of empirical propositions of which it is permissible to

---

[10] This is the example used in the preface to the second edition of *LTL*, p. 15.

[11] 'Strong and Weak Verification', *Mind* (1939). The paper is reprinted in M. Lazerowitz, *The Structure of Metaphysics*.

say that they can be verified conclusively'. The class in question was that of 'basic propositions' — propositions about which 'it is impossible to be mistaken . . . except in a verbal sense' (*LTL* p. 13). Examples of such propositions were 'I am in pain', and 'This is green' when used 'merely to designate a sense-datum' being experienced at the time of speaking.[12] Such propositions, he now maintained, were verifiable in the strong sense.

In a further paper, however, Lazerowitz pointed out that Ayer's strong and weak senses of 'verify' were both at odds with the ordinary sense of that word.[13] For where Ayer spoke of strong verification, for example in reference to 'I am in pain', one would not normally speak of verification at all. On the other hand, where he spoke of verification in a 'weak' sense (yielding no more than a probability of truth), there we would use the word in a straightforward and unqualified way — for example in verifying that someone is at the door.

One cannot in normal conditions, be said to verify that one is in pain, because verification presupposes a possibility of doubt. To verify is to find out whether (or, according to another usage, to check that) a statement is true. If it makes no sense to speak of doubt, then it makes no sense to speak of verification either. The connection between verification and the possibility of doubt was recognised by Schlick, who, however, went on to claim that one could speak of doubting one's own pain. 'I can quite meaningfully ask, for example (in the course, say, of a physiological experiment): Do I now actually feel pain or not?' (*GA* p. 105, *PP* p. 276, *ER* p. 101.) Schlick was right in seeing the need for such a claim from the verificationist point of view. And perhaps it would be possible to describe circumstances in which the question 'Am I at this moment feeling a pain?' would really make sense. But in normal conditions the question does not make sense. Nor does it make sense, therefore, to speak, in such conditions, of verification.

---

[12] See 'Verification and Experience', *Proceedings of the Aristotelian Society,* XXXVII, reprinted in *LP*; and *The Foundations of Empirical Knowledge* p. 81.

[13] 'Strong and Weak Verification II', *Mind* (1950); reprinted in Lazerowitz, *The Structure of Metaphysics.*

The same comments apply to Ayer's example 'This is green'. Of course it is possible to be in doubt, and hence to verify, whether some ordinary object is green. But this, as we saw, was not the way in which Ayer meant his example. The statement was supposed 'merely to designate a sense-datum' and to be, therefore, beyond the possibility of mistake. This was what made it verifiable in the 'strong' sense — which, if the above comments are correct, is not a normal sense at all. It remains unclear, then, what Ayer meant by 'verification' and 'verifiability'. Perhaps it would be better to regard his criterion as being about the deducibility of a certain type of statement — an observation-statement or 'experiential proposition'.

Further difficulties arise in trying to operate Ayer's test so as to achieve the separation of metaphysics from science. As we saw, what was required as 'the mark of a genuine factual proposition' was that from this proposition, when conjoined with 'certain other premises', it must be possible to deduce 'some experiential propositions'. It did not take Ayer's critics long to find ways of assembling propositions and premises so as to produce silly results. An example was given by Ayer himself in his introduction to the second edition.

> Thus, the statements 'the Absolute is lazy' and 'if the Absolute is lazy, this is white' jointly entail the observation-statement 'this is white', and since 'this is white' does not follow from either of these premises, taken by itself, both of them satisfy my criterion of meaning. (*LTL* p. 15.)[14]

To meet the difficulty Ayer put forward a modified version of his criterion, the main purport of which was to stipulate that the 'other premise' must itself consist of an observation-statement or statements. This was intended to prevent statements like 'The Absolute is lazy' from appearing among the premises. But Carl Hempel argued that such measures

---

[14] Ayer's example shows that he had strict deduction in mind, as I assumed on page 39. But it remains difficult to see how the example given there could be treated as one of strict deduction, as is the case in the passage just quoted.

could not prevent the criterion from producing absurd results. The new criterion, he said, 'allows empirical significance to any conjunction S.N, where S satisfies Ayer's criterion while N is a sentence such as "The absolute is perfect", which is to be disqualified by that criterion'.[15] Hempel's point was that if statement S has the right entailments (those that enable it to satisfy Ayer's criterion), then the conjunction S.N must have them too, for whatever is entailed by S is also entailed by S conjoined with any other statement. Thus it will always be possible for a nonsensical statement N to get through on the same ticket, so to speak, as the *bona fide* statement S with which it has been conjoined for just this purpose.

Further attempts were made to amend Ayer's criterion so as to eliminate nonsensical components. This led to formulations of considerable complexity, which will not be discussed here.[16] A different view was taken, however, by David Rynin, who argued that the objections of Hempel and Church were misconceived.[17] Since N is to denote a piece of nonsense (a pseudo-statement) it cannot, argued Rynin, stand in logical relations such as those of conjunction and entailment, as assumed in Hempel's argument. 'If as Hempel seems to take for granted, we already know that "The absolute is perfect" is meaningless . . . then what right have we to treat it as a premise in an argument and attempt to draw conclusions from it alone or in conjunction with other sentences? ('Vindication' p. 59). Rynin concluded that the very identification of an 'N' component (i.e. one that was unverifiable) would be

[15] 'Problems and Changes in the Empiricist Criterion of Meaning', in *Revue Internationale de Philosophie* (1950), reprinted in *LP*; also see the revised version in section 4 of *Aspects of Scientific Explanation*. Hempel used the standard logical symbol '.' to mean 'and', so that 'S.N' denotes a conjunction of statements. An objection similar to Hempel's was made by Alonzo Church in his review of Ayer's book in the *Journal of Symbolic Logic* (1949).

[16] See, e.g., D. J. O'Connor, 'Some Consequences of Professor Ayer's Verification Principle', *Analysis* (1949–50), and R. Brown and J. Watling, 'Amending the Verification Principle', *Analysis* (1950–51).

[17] 'Vindication of L*G*C*L P*S*T*V*SM', in *Proceedings and Addresses of the American Philosophical Association* (1957). Hempel conceded the point to Rynin when his papers were reprinted in Ayer (ed.), *Logical Positivism* and Hempel, *Aspects of Scientific Explanation*.

enough to eliminate the whole statement of which it was a component. He took himself, accordingly, to have 'vindicated' the criterion of verifiability.[18]

Now a reader not familiar with propositional logic may be puzzled by this dispute. He may feel that the obvious comment about Hempel's S.N is that part of it is meaningful and part of it not; and that there is no need to pursue the question in regard to S.N as a whole. Nevertheless the dispute draws attention to a basic weakness in Ayer's approach. As we have seen, Ayer's criterion was one of deducibility: a statement T would pass if at least one observation-statement O were deducible from it. But clearly O would not be the whole of the meaning of T. What happens, then, about the rest? May not T contain an N component as part of its meaning – or intended meaning? This is possible, whatever we may say about the logical relations of N, and whether or not we agree with Rynin about the meaningfulness of T as a whole. But in order to identify N, we must examine the whole meaning (or intended meaning) of N; we need analysis and not merely deduction.

We should not expect, however, that analysis will be a simple matter. As Rynin pointed out, we cannot tell in the abstract whether a statement such as 'The absolute is perfect' is meaningful or not according to the criterion of verifiability, any more than we can tell this about the nuclear physicist's talk about 'anti-matter'. To arrive at an answer we must, said Rynin, speak to the person using the language in question and elicit from him what truth-conditions (if any) he attaches to his statements; a process which may call for patience and understanding ('Vindication' pp. 56–7). To this we may add that even an ordinary statement like 'The postman is at the door', though seemingly innocent of non-observable components, may prove no less difficult. For one thing, the word 'postman' implies an institution with rules and norms; and secondly, it may be thought that the word 'man' includes the idea of an unobservable entity, namely an immaterial soul. And, as we shall see, various problems arise about the analysis of even simpler statements.

---

[18] His own version of the criterion is given in 'Vindication', p. 53.

In putting forward his 'weak' criterion, Ayer may have seemed to be providing a way of determining whether a statement is meaningful without the need for a full analysis of its meaning. But this advantage turns out to be illusory. In this matter the new empiricism must follow in the footsteps of the old. The latter is sometimes defined as the view that all our knowledge is 'derived from' or 'based on' sense-experience. But these phrases must be understood in a suitably strong sense. Kant began his *Critique of Pure Reason* by conceding that 'all our knowledge begins with experience', but his aim was to show that there is more to it than that. Conversely, when an empiricist claims that all knowledge is derived from experience, he must mean that there is *no* more to it; that it is wholly constituted by experience. If he meant merely that experience is a necessary condition of knowledge, then he would not be excluding other factors — such as the 'innate ideas' rejected by Locke — from being necessary conditions as well. The distinctive claim of empiricism must be, and has been, not merely that knowledge is dependent on experience in some way or other, but that it is wholly constituted by experience. (What this means is explained in the writings of such empiricists as Locke and Hume.)

Similarly, the Logical Empiricist must be saying that the meaning of statements is wholly constituted by the relevant observation-statements and not merely that some of the latter are deducible; and this calls for analysis. Now as we saw in chapter 1 (page 11) analysis had indeed been the general approach of the Logical Empiricists. It was thought that a statement must be analysable by the truth-functional method into observation-statements, and that this analysis would show what exactly its meaning was. Some of the difficulties of this programme will be discussed in the next chapter.

4 Analysis

4.1 ANALYSIS AND PHENOMENA

The idea of analysis is one that arises naturally enough from a consideration of concepts and statements. When we read, for example, that 'Wittgenstein found this letter in Otterthal on his return from the Christmas holidays and replied (7th January 1925) in the most friendly terms, saying that he did *not* have a copy of the *Tractatus*',[1] it is obvious that we have here a complex statement which could be broken down into components having various logical relations to one another. It was sometimes maintained by Logical Empiricists that, after the elimination of metaphysics, analysis remained as the proper task of philosophers. According to Carnap, philosophy should be seen as an adjunct to science; its business was 'the clarification of the statements of empirical science', and this would be brought about by 'the step by step reduction of concepts to more fundamental concepts and of statements to more fundamental statements'.[2]

The old empiricists, as we saw in chapter 1, used analysis (albeit in a psychological sense) to account for ideas that we may have of things not within our experience. Thus, according to Hume, the idea of a golden mountain is made up of ideas of things with which we have been 'formerly acquainted'. The new empiricists, as I have said, thought of analysis as terminating in observation-statements; and of the latter as being verifiable by corresponding acts of verification. 'To analyse a proposition', we read in Waismann's 'Theses', 'means to consider how it is to be verified. Language *touches* reality with elementary propositions' (*WWK* p. 249).

---

[1] *WWK* p. 13, editor's introduction. The letter was from Schlick.

[2] 'The Old and the New Logic', *Erkenntnis*, vol. I (1930–31); *LP* p. 133.

But what form would these 'elementary propositions' take? It might be thought that they would be simple, ordinary statements about ordinary objects in one's vicinity. But this was not how the matter was regarded in the 'Theses'.

> It is clear that assertions about bodies (tables, chairs, are not elementary propositions. Indeed, no one would believe that in speaking of bodies we have reached the final elements of description. What elementary propositions describe are: phenomena (experiences). (*WWK* p. 249.)

According to the 'Theses', statements about tables and chairs are based on statements about experiences or phenomena. The latter, by contrast, are not based on any further statements; and this is what makes them 'elementary' in the scheme of analysis.

> I can certainly say: 'This conductor is electrically charged, *because* the electroscope displays a deflection.' But I cannot say: 'This patch in my visual field is yellow, *because* . . .'. If, in order to verify a proposition, I can no longer appeal to other propositions, then this indicates that the proposition is elementary. (*WWK* p. 249.)

The ultimate step in the process of verification must consist, on this view, in *having* the experience described by the elementary proposition (such as 'This patch in my visual field is yellow'). This view is akin to Ayer's idea of 'strong' verification, as discussed on pp. 39—40. Ayer, as we saw, thought that such statements as 'I am in pain' and 'This is green' — when used 'merely to designate a sense-datum' — could be 'verified conclusively', by merely having the experience concerned. A difficulty about this view (as we saw) was that it goes against the normal connection of verification with possibility of doubt. There is also a difference between it and what we understood by verification in chapter 2, when discussing the verification principle and 'the method' of verification. As was pointed out on page 18, a method is a way of doing something. And this is in keeping with what we ordinarily understand by verification; for to verify a statement is to take some action to find out whether (or confirm that) the statement is true. But on the view now before us, verification is a passive matter. It consists in having an experience or being aware of 'phenomena', such as a yellow patch in one's visual field, and not in any *act* of verification, such as, say, looking in the next room to verify that the carpet is yellow.

It may be doubted whether it is correct to speak of verification in this passive sense. And indeed, the view now before us, though generally held by verificationists, is more usually known as 'phenomenalism'. On the other hand, this version of verificationism (phenomenalism) is not exposed to the difficulty mentioned at the end of section 2.2, in connection with Schlick's talk of a method of verification. We noticed there that there is not a close enough correspondence between meaning and method of verification, since a given method of verification (e.g. looking at the carpet) will be appropriate to more than one statement. This difficulty does not arise with the present version because, according to it, an elementary statement is verified by having just the experience that the statement 'describes'; so that 'This patch in my visual field is yellow' will have a different verification from 'This patch in my visual field is blue'.

But what is the logical relation between such statements and statements about bodily objects? From the fact that there is, say, a yellow table in the room it would not follow that anyone is having the relevant experience, for there may not be anyone there to see it. It was early recognized by phenomenalists that the analysis must consist largely of hypotheticals – statements about what *would* be experienced in suitable circumstances. Such a view had already been taken by the empiricist John Stuart Mill in his *System of Logic* of 1843. To speak of the existence of an absent thing was, he maintained, merely to express 'our conviction that we should perceive it on a certain supposition, namely, if we were in the needful circumstances of time and place, and endowed with the needful perfection of organs'. In another work he claimed that 'Matter . . . may be defined, a Permanent Possibility of Sensation'.[3]

---

[3] *A System of Logic,* III. 24.1, and *An Examination of Sir William Hamilton's Philosophy,* p. 233.

But in what sense would the truth of the hypothetical statement follow from the fact that there is a yellow table in the room? Not in the sense of strict logic, as required by the system of truth-functional analysis. Even if I am in the room, and endowed with normal eyesight, I may fail to see the table. The point is perhaps more obvious with such statements as 'There is a button in this drawer' and 'There is a needle in the haystack'; but there are also some obvious reasons why one may fail to see the table. One may, for example, be looking the wrong way, or have one's attention diverted. To some extent these possibilities can be met by inserting suitable stipulations into the analysis. But one could never be sure that all conceivable reasons had been covered. It is, after all, a familiar experience in courts of law that a witness has failed to see something which he was, apparently, in a good position to see; or that two such witnesses give conflicting reports. In any case, there could not be a strict entailment from a statement about the presence of a table to statements about what anyone sees.

There is also a failure of entailment in the other direction. It is true that the presence of a table would be entailed by the truth of 'I see a table'. But as we saw in the quotation from Waismann, this was not the sort of statement that was regarded as 'elementary'. It could not be so, since the statement that there is a table there can itself be regarded as part of the analysis of 'I see a table'. The point of introducing statements about 'phenomena' and 'experiences' was, precisely, that such a statement would *not* entail the existence of a bodily object, but would be confined to something that is happening to the person concerned. Nevertheless it was thought that statements about tables and chairs must be analysable into statements about experiences. (It should be noticed that 'experience' is here being used in a rather unusual sense. Normally if we ask someone to describe his experiences, we would not expect him to reply in terms of patches in his visual field.)

But what logical link could there be from such statements to statements about bodily objects? We need not, of course, confine ourselves to statements about one person's experiences; those of others can also be brought in. Again, we need not assume that we are confined to statements about coloured patches, other sorts of descriptions may also be included. Suppose, then, that all this is done. Will it follow from the whole set of experiential statements that there is a table there? It is true that as we include more and more experiential statements (bringing in, so to speak, more and more witnesses) the chances of its not being there will become infinitesimal; but still this will not amount to strict entailment. There would be no formal contradiction in supposing that there is no table there in spite of experiential statements to the contrary.

This failure of entailment led the verificationists to maintain that ordinary statements about tables and chairs are not, or not conclusively, verifiable. Wittgenstein spoke of such statements as 'hypotheses' which could not be 'definitely verified'. This did not mean, he added, that there is for them a verification 'which one may approach more and more closely without ever reaching it'. It meant, rather, that 'a hypothesis has a different formal relation to reality from that of verification'. On the other hand, 'the point of talking about sense-data and immediate experience is that we want a description that is not hypothetical'.[4]

Verificationists tried in various ways to come to terms with the conclusion that ordinary statements are not verifiable, trying to show that this failure is not culpable as in the case of metaphysics. Some of these attempts will be discussed in the following sections. There is, however, another way in which the analysis into statements about 'immediate experience' is paradoxical. These statements, we are to understand, are peculiarly close to the source of meaning of all statements, being directly descriptive of items of verification. One might have thought, then, that we could have the meanings of other statements explained to us in terms of these. And in general this is what one might expect of an analysis of meaning. (This was also our concern at the end of the last chapter.) But will the proposed analysis serve this purpose? Ayer claimed that such analysis 'serves to increase our understand-

---

[4]*PB* pp. 282–5. Also see *WWK* p. 97, 'Verification and the Immediately Given'. The idea of 'conclusive verification' will be further discussed in section 4.4.

ing of the sentences in which we refer to material things'
(*LTL* p. 91).[5] He condeded, however, that there is 'a sense in
which we already understand such sentences'. But this con-
cession does not go far enough. If there is something here
that we understand only 'in a sense', it is not the sentence
'Here is a table', but the talk about sense-data and immediate
experience. One may understand the former without understanding, or properly understanding, the latter; but not vice
versa. The description of sense-data has, after all, to be done
in the same terms as those applied to material objects. Some
analysts have spoken of sense-data 'of a table', etc.; others
have spoken of yellow patches and the like. But either way,
we can understand these descriptions only because we are
familiar with their use in describing ordinary objects.

4.2 GENERALITY

If the analysis into experiential statements could be straightforwardly completed, then it would provide a clear-cut deter-
mination of meaning; showing precisely which are the
meaningful components of any given statement. In fact, however, verificationists have had continually to face the twin
problems of inclusion and exclusion: of applying their
principle in such a way as to condone statements about tables
and chairs and statements of science, while eliminating statements of metaphysics and theology.

The problem of inclusion arises in a particularly striking
way with general statements. It does so even if 'verify' is used
in the ordinary and not the phenomenalist sense. Consider
the statement 'John is wearing a tie'. In the ordinary sense, I
can verify this by a single observation. Similarly, I can verify
the statement that all the men in this room are wearing ties,
by observing them one by one. This statement, we may say,
is equivalent to the conjunction 'John is wearing a tie and
James is wearing a tie . . .' and so on until all the men in the
room have been enumerated.

[5] In *Language, Truth and Logic* Ayer advocated the analysis of statements (phenomenalism) as well as stressing the advantages of his 'weak' criterion, as discussed in
section 3.2. He later gave up the former while adhering to the latter.

But it is a different matter when the statement is an 'open-ended' one, such as 'All men are mortal'. The 'all men' in this case is not analysable into a finite conjunction of names; nor does the truth of the statement follow from the verification of any finite number of instances. It is, in that sense, unverifiable. Similarly, the meaning of 'Water expands below 4°C' is not confined to a given number of instances; its meaning goes beyond any finite number of observations.

For the Logical Positivists this gap between meaning and verification was especially serious. For they regarded science as the paradigm of meaningful discourse. Philosophy, they thought, could be made respectable only by turning it into a branch of science. Yet general statements of the infinite kind are typical of the laws of science.

A solution of this problem was offered by Schlick in his 'Causality in present-day Physics' of 1931. 'A law of nature', he wrote, 'does not basically have the logical character of a "statement"; it represents, rather, an "instruction for the forming of statements".'[6] A genuine statement, he maintained, must be 'conclusively verifiable'; and this was not true of laws of nature, but only of the particular statements formed under these 'instructions'; statements like 'Under these and these circumstances this pointer will indicate this line on the scale' (*GA* pp. 55–7). In the case of the laws (as with any instruction), there could be a question of usefulness but not of verification (*GA* p. 67).

This view is, however, at odds with ordinary ideas of what it is to believe and to use a general (law-like) statement. Someone who believes that all *A*'s are *B* believes that this is a true statement and not that it is a useful instruction; and in telling me that all *A*'s are *B* he is telling me that something is the case and not giving me an instruction.

In another passage, however, we find the claim that a 'genuine statement' must be 'conclusively verifiable *or falsifiable*' (*GA* p. 67, italics added). Here Schlick seems not to have noticed that the problem of infinity does not arise in falsifying (as opposed to verifying) a general statement; for a

---

[6] *GA* p. 57, *PP* p. 176 ff. On *GA* p. 55 there is a similar claim about causal statements. Schlick abandoned these views in later writings, however.

single observation of an A that is not B would suffice to show that 'All A's are B' is false. Karl Popper had adopted falsifiability as a 'criterion of demarcation' for genuine science; 'it must be possible', he maintained, 'for an empirical scientific system to be refuted by experience'.[7] Some of the Logical Positivists came to believe that falsification rather than verification should be the main concept in their account of meaning.

This idea has its limitations, however. In the first place, falsifiability is suitable as a criterion of meaningfulness rather than as an account of meaning (as the verification principle had been). It may answer the question 'Is this statement meaningful?', but not 'What does its meaning consist in?'. Thus it would not be a replacement for the original combination of the verification principle and the criterion of verifiability.

Secondly, there is a type of statement where falsifiability would not give the desired result.[8] The difficulty here is a sort of mirror-image of the one about general statements. If the verification of 'All A's are B' requires an infinite number of observations, then the same will be true of the *falsification* of '*Some A*'s are B'. Consider the statement that there are yetis. It says, in effect, that some animals have these and these features. We may observe any number of animals and find that they do not have these features; but this would not mean that no animal has them – that the statement has been falsified. This type of statement is, however, well served by the criterion of verifiability; for a single positive observation would suffice to verify it.[9]

A way of dealing with the problem would be to include both verifiability and falsifiability in the criterion of meaningfulness.[10] It would seem in any case that both must play a role. Consider the statement 'There are no yetis'. This a

---

[7] *The Logic of Scientific Discovery*, p. 41.

[8] See, e.g., the paper by Hempel mentioned on page 42.

[9] That is, assuming that 'some' = 'at least one'. Otherwise two positive observations would do the trick.

[10] Such a criterion was formulated by Rynin; see the note on page 43.

general statement, albeit a negative one. It is unverifiable in the same sense as 'All men are mortal', since its truth would not be entailed by any finite number of instances. But it would be paradoxical to declare 'There are yetis' to be meaningful (because verifiable) while describing its contradictory, 'There are no yetis', as meaningless (because not verifiable). A similar paradox would result, vice versa, if falsifiability alone were used.

4.3 'POSITIVISM' AND 'REALISM'

To resort to falsifiability as a criterion of meaningfulness is (as I pointed out) to abandon one of the main ideas of verificationism — that meaning is somehow identical with verification, and that the question 'What is meaning?' (and not merely 'Which statements are meaningful?') can be answered by reference to verification. This was the view to which Schlick adhered. In his 'Positivism and Realism' (1932), he spoke of 'the identity of meaning and verification' (though in this paper, as we shall see, he understood the term in the phenomenalist rather than in the active sense). A statement, he insisted, 'has a meaning only in so far as it can be verified; it only *signifies* what is verified and absolutely *nothing* beyond this'. He admitted, however, that there was no end to the number of items of verification relevant to an ordinary statement. How then could its meaning be identified with 'the method of verification'? The answer, according to Schlick, was simply to accept that the meaning and verification of a statement are infinite. 'The meaning of every physical statement ultimately lies always in an endless chain of data.' But how, in that case, can we be sure that a given statement is, or is wholly, meaningful? Schlick's answer consisted in a challenge.

> If anyone thinks that the meaning of a proposition is not in fact exhausted by what can be verified in the given, but extends far beyond that, then he must at least admit that this surplus of meaning is utterly indescribable, unstatable in any way, and inexpressible by any language. For let him just try to state it!

If he does so, argued Schlick, he will find that his additional statement will merely be describing some further conditions (overlooked, perhaps, in the analysis so far) which can in their turn be 'verified in the given'. (*GA* pp. 93–6, *PP* pp. 266–9, *ER* pp. 91–4.)

In his equation of meaning with verification, Schlick differs, on the one hand, from those verificationists who renounced the question 'What is meaning?' and, on the other hand, from those who tried to answer it by means of a formal and finite analysis. Schlick offers no such analysis, and thereby avoids the difficulties of this enterprise; but he is confident that any additional component of meaning that may be mentioned will be covered by a corresponding item of verification.

Schlick's idea may be illustrated by the kind of example discussed in the last section. The meaning of 'All A's are B' goes, apparently, beyond any possible method of verification; the former being infinite and the latter finite. Schlick's answer is, in effect, to deny the second point; for he speaks, as we saw, of 'an endless concatenation of data'. Thus if someone points out that the meaning of 'All A's' is not exhausted by the 1,000 A's observed so far, then Schlick can answer that the same is true of the method of verification; but that in stating the 'additional meaning', i.e. that going beyond the 1,000 A's, the objector has also given the corresponding method of verification, namely observation of further A's.

In this paper, however, Schlick dealt with particular rather than general statements. As we saw in section 4.1, the former were also held to be not verifiable, or not conclusively so. It was, indeed, commonly argued that the problem of infinity was essentially the same in both cases.[11] Schlick's main con-

---

[11] 'There is no fundamental difference between a universal sentence and a particular sentence with regard to verifiability but only a difference in degree. Take for instance the following sentence: "There is a white sheet of paper on this table." . . . Here as well as in the case of the law, we try to examine sentences which we infer from the sentence in question. These inferred sentences are predictions about future observations. The number of such predictions which we can derive from the sentence given is infinite, and therefore the sentence can never be completely verified.' (Carnap, *TM* p. 48.) This passage will be critically examined in section 4.4.

cern, however, was not about infinity, but about the equation of statements about physical objects with statements about experiences. He maintained that 'the claim that a thing is real is a statement about lawful connections of experiences' (*GA* p. 103, *PP* p. 274, *ER* p. 99).

Now even if the reader accepts Schlick's way of disposing of the problem of infinity, he may feel that a regular connection of experiences cannot possibly be equated with the existence of a physical object. It seems obvious that experiences and tables and chairs are things of very different kinds; and that to affirm the existence of one is very different from affirming the existence of the other. Perhaps the reader will want to say that a physical object is the *cause* of suitable experiences; but that it exists independently of them.

Is Schlick denying that the world contains physical objects as distinct from experiences? No. He emphasized that his view was not the 'positivism' which he found in certain earlier philosophers. He was not claiming, he said, that 'only the given exists'.[12] 'Anyone who asserts this principle thereby attempts to advance a claim that is metaphysical in the same sense, and to the same degree, as the seemingly opposite contention, "There is a transcendent reality" − i.e. a reality other than experience' (*GA* p. 87, *PP* p. 261, *ER* pp. 85−6). The very meanings of 'real' and 'exist' are, according to Schlick, tied to experience; hence it is no less nonsensical to deny than to affirm that there exists anything other than that.

But Schlick's main effort was directed against the 'realist' rather than against the 'positivist'. According to the former, said Schlick,

the meaning of a reality-statement is by no means exhausted in mere assertions of the form 'Under these particular circumstances this particular experience will occur' (where these assertions, on our view, are in any case an infinite multitude); the meaning, he says, in fact lies *beyond this* in something else, which must be referred to, say, as 'independent existence', 'transcendent being' or the like,

---

[12] German 'Es gibt nur das Gegebene'. Schlick drew attention to the play of words here.

and of which our principle [the verification principle] provides no account (*GA* p. 111, *PP* p. 280, *ER* p. 106).

Like the eighteenth-century empiricist Berkeley, Schlick was concerned to reassure the reader that his account did not in any way diminish the reality of the familiar world. Having rejected the talk of a transcendent reality, he was, he said, left with 'the same world as that of everybody else; it lacks nothing that is needed in order to make meaningful all the statements of science and all the actions of daily life'. He merely refused 'to add meaningless statements to his description of the world' (*GA* p. 113, *PP* p. 282, *ER* pp. 107–8).

Schlick's repeated assurances are a sign of uneasiness. The realist – or as we may as well say, the ordinary reader – will not so easily get over his feeling that there is something wrong with Schlick's equation. But where does the fault lie? The problem, as here set up, seems intractable. Either, it seems, we must give up the distinction between physical objects and experiences, or we must hold that in speaking about tables and chairs we are speaking about a reality that transcends experience, thus provoking the appellations 'realist' and 'metaphysician'.

This is not a problem that arises with other, 'ordinary' cases of metaphysics. Take, for example, the belief in a transcendent God; or the claim that there must be universal entities in another world, to give meaning to the universal words we use in this world. Someone who makes these claims will not be surprised, let alone embarrassed, at being called a metaphysician. To speak of a reality beyond experience was what he intended. But the realist in Schlick's case has no such intention. He does not want to set up as a defender of metaphysics. That is why Schlick can be confident in issuing his challenge 'Let him state this additional meaning!'. A metaphysician would answer this by speaking of a transcendental meaning, taking issue with Schlick about his right to do so. But what is the realist to say?

Perhaps the realist will think that the way to maintain his view is by pointing to the lack of entailment between experiences and physical objects. Is it not possible, in any given case, that the reality of a thing will turn out to be different from our experiences of it? But if he takes this line, Schlick will be ready for him. For to say that a thing may turn out to be different is (he will reply) merely to say something about possible further experiences.

Yet if we return to ordinary talk about experience and about tables and chairs, it may be hard to see how the realist's problem could ever arise. Using the terms in their ordinary senses, it is correct to say that tables and chairs are things within our experience, and yet to maintain the distinction between talk about furniture and talk about experience. What has gone wrong?

The difficulty arises because Schlick thinks of 'experience' in the phenomenalist sense — as something that is 'given' to a passive subject. This may be satisfactory if we think of such experiences as a feeling of nausea or a sensation in one's leg. Empiricists have thought, however, that our experience of the external world is essentially of the same kind, the difference being merely that in this case we have 'sense-experience' — something (a 'sense-datum') being given to the senses, or to us via the senses. Now it may be admitted, again, that something happens to us in our perception of the world. But there is more than this to perception and to experience. If we think purely in terms of something happening to a passive subject, then we shall not be able to do justice to the sense of reality with which Schlick was trying to cope. We can, however, do something towards closing the gap by taking 'experience' in a broader sense than that imposed on it by the empiricist view.

'Under these particular circumstances this particular experience will occur.' This was the type of statement which, according to Schlick, constitutes the meaning of a statement asserting the reality of a thing (above, page 55). Now we have already noted (page 46) that verification, as ordinarily understood, involves activity. To know the method of verification of a statement may mean knowing how to *bring about* the conditions that Schlick speaks of, as opposed to merely waiting for them to happen. I may, for example, have to go into the other room and look, in order to verify the existence of a table. If the verification principle is taken so as to include these 'active' aspects, then it will be more plausible than otherwise. But supposing I have done what is necessary in order to see the table (and that I do have that experience): does this complete the active part of the method of verification?

When, as we are told, Jesus rose from the dead, various people had experiences of seeing and hearing him; and perhaps anyone present would have had similar experiences. But Doubting Thomas could not believe until he had touched. Touching is, so to speak, nearer to reality than seeing and hearing. Seeing and hearing are the senses we usually think of first and most prominently when thinking of sense-perception. But touching is more decisive in establishing the reality of a thing – assuming that we are speaking of tangible things. Sometimes, indeed, we feel that only what is tangible really exists. A rainbow, for example, has a certain permanence and can be seen by anyone suitably placed. Yet it would not be altogether wrong to say of a rainbow that there is nothing really there. (One might perhaps say this in explanation to a child.) The point of saying this is that the visual phenomena of the rainbow are not backed by a tangible reality; we cannot confirm our vision of the rainbow by touching it. In this sense tables and chairs exist, while rainbows do not. (There is also, of course, a sense in which they do.)

But what is so special about touch? Is not touch just another mode of sense-experience in addition to hearing and vision? Using my sense of sight, I perceive that this object is brown and square; using my sense of touch, that it is cold and smooth. If we think of touch in this way, then we shall merely have added some more items to the phenomenalist's analysis: items of touch in addition to those of the other senses. But we shall have done little to close the gap between experience and reality which so much worried Schlick's realist (and, as is evident, Schlick himself). The importance of touch does not lie, however, in feeling that a thing is cold, smooth and the like, but in establishing its solidity. But is this not, again, just another item of sense-experience? No; for it is not essentially a matter of feeling, as in the case of feeling that something is smooth or cold. What matters in the case of solidity is that, when applying my hand to the object, there are certain things I can and cannot *do*. I *cannot* pass my

hand through a table or a man's body; I *can* grip a physical
object and perhaps pick it up. I cannot put one physical object where another is; nor can I put myself into that place.
These are, in some sense, facts of experience; but not in the
empiricist's sense of something that is 'given' to a passive
subject.

It is worth observing how some of the older empiricists
tried to come to terms with the idea of solidity. Hume rightly
saw the question as one of 'impenetrability'. 'A man, who has
the palsey in one hand, has as perfect an idea of impenetrability, when he observes that hand to be supported by the
table, as when he feels the same table with the other hand.'[13]
Hume has correctly noted that a sense of feeling is not required in order to establish that a thing is solid. But he has
merely replaced this sense by another: that by which 'he
observes that hand to be supported by the table' — presumably the sense of sight.

In Locke's *Essay* we find some remarks which may seem
closer to the 'active' account that I have given. 'Let him put a
flint or a football between his hands, and then endeavour to
join them, and he will know' (2.4.6). This is Locke's answer
to someone who asks what solidity is. But the resemblance to
my account is only apparent. For Locke insists that our idea
of solidity is purely a matter of 'sensation'; we have it
because 'we always feel something' (2.4.1). Thus the essential
thing about putting a flint or football between my hands is
not the discovery that there is something I cannot do (i.e.
join my hands), it is the *feeling* that this endeavour produces
in my hands.[14]

Now if, contrary to the empiricist–phenomenalist view,
we include under 'experience' the facts about our inter-
actions with solid objects, then we may be less inclined to see
a gap between experience and 'the reality of a thing'. What
does it mean to say that there is a table in the corner? It

---

[13] *Treatise* 1.4.4; ed. Selby-Bigge p. 230.

[14] Locke also spoke of the impenetrability of bodies to one another. But our observation of this must again, according to him, be a matter of passive 'sensation',
in accordance with his system.

means, replies the phenomenalist, that if anyone were looking in that corner, he would have an experience of seeing a
table. But it is easy to suppose that this statement is true and
yet there is no table there. Perhaps the phenomenalist will try
to close the gap by bringing in more experiences of the passive kind. But if he wants to do justice to our sense of reality,
he will also have to talk about activity and contact. If this
were done, then the 'realist' would not feel so strongly that
something − the essential thing − had been left out. Or if he
does, then perhaps he really is trying to say something metaphysical, as Schlick supposed. But assuming this is not the
case, should he (and we) now agree with Schlick that 'the
claim that a thing is real is a statement about lawful connections of experiences'?

It is hardly to be expected that assertions about tables and
chairs could be replaced by statements regarding experiences.
This is not merely because of the problem of infinity, discussed at the start of the present section. The point is that, in
speaking of our perception of ordinary objects (things within
our experience, as we might say), we do *not* speak of 'experiences' of them. To speak of an experience of seeing a table is
to employ a rather unusual expression; one that implies
something different from, and at odds with, an ordinary case
of seeing a table and asserting that it is there. If there is a
'realist' problem about such assertions, then it must be dealt
with, not by adopting a new and potentially misleading
vocabulary, but by achieving a correct understanding of what
is, and what is not, involved in such assertions.

4.4 VERIFICATION AND 'COMPLETE VERIFICATION'

Schlick's 'realist', as we saw, felt that a statement about a
physical object means more than the relevant experiences.
There is another way, however, in which it may be thought
to mean less. We have seen that, according to Schlick, the
'data' which make up the verification of such a statement are
'endless'. He inferred from this that 'in the last resort such a
proposition can never be proved absolutely true' (*GA* p. 95,

PP 268, *ER* 93).[15] But it may be objected that in saying, for example, that there is a table in the corner, one would be making a finite (and indeed rather modest) claim. Thus the 'verification' of the statement would seem to go far beyond its meaning.

But is it true that the verification is infinite? Schlick thought of it as embracing *all* the observations, made by anyone at any time, which would be relevant to the truth of the statement. But this is not what we ordinarily mean by verification. If I want to verify that there is a table in the corner, I need only to go and look.

It was, however, generally accepted among verificationists that ordinary statements about tables and chairs are not, or not completely, verifiable. We saw in section 3.2 how this view led Ayer to put forward his 'weak' criterion. Carnap put the matter as follows:

> There is no fundamental difference between a universal sentence and a particular sentence with regard to verifiability but only a difference in degree. Take for instance the following sentence: 'There is a white sheet of paper on this table.' . . . Here as well as in the case of the law, we try to examine sentences which we infer from the sentence in question. These inferred sentences are predictions about future observations. The number of such predictions which we can derive from the sentence given is infinite; and therefore the sentence can never be completely verified. (*TM* p. 48.)[16]

Now for this argument to be valid, the phrase 'completely verify' would have to mean 'examine an infinite number of predictions about future observations'. Does it mean this?

To speak of verification as complete or incomplete is not always appropriate. We do so where verification can be seen as consisting of parts; for example, in verifying a set of

[15] Perhaps the 'absolutely' was meant to qualify 'proved' rather than 'true'.

[16] Previously quoted in section 4.3. For further discussion of this passage and the idea of 'complete verification', see 'The Verification Argument' in Norman Malcolm's *Knowledge and Certainty*.

figures or a story told by a witness in court. But in these cases the difference between complete and incomplete is not that between infinite and finite. To say that one has completely verified a set of figures or a long story is not to say that one has completed an infinite number of operations.

But to verify that there is a white sheet of paper on this table is not, in the normal case, something that admits of degrees. I do not verify this statement 'completely' or 'incompletely'; I just verify it or do not verify it, as the case may be. And in order to verify it I do not need to infer all the observation-statements that might be inferred from it. A single observation is probably all that is needed. Anyone who denies this must be using 'verify' in an abnormal way.

A similar misconception of verification occurs in the following passage:

> It needs no sceptic to be convinced that you cannot verify today a statement about an event tomorrow. However the signs may point to an event, call it X, occurring tomorrow, it is always at least logically possible that it will not occur.[17]

Here the author explicitly claims that his use of words is the normal one: 'it needs no sceptic', he says, to accept his conclusion. But to make the argument valid, the phrase 'verify that X will occur' must be taken to mean 'find it logically impossible that X will not occur'. And this is not what it normally means. Hospers is right in assuming that the latter condition cannot be fulfilled, but this has little bearing on the question of verifying that X will occur. I can, for example, verify that an eclipse of the moon will take place on 29 August, by consulting an almanac. But that does not mean that its non-occurrence is logically impossible. I can also verify, by enquiring at the station, that my train will leave at 7.35 tomorrow morning. Of course I can easily think of circumstances (strikes, derailments and the like) in which the train would not leave then, in spite of my verification. But this does not mean that I used the word 'verify' wrongly; on

[17] John Hospers, *Introduction to Philosophical Analysis*, p. 198.

the contrary, it would have been wrong not to use it. Again, if my guest asks me to verify that his train will leave at such and such a time, I cannot complain that his request is unintelligible or his use of 'verify' improper.

There is also a misconception in Carnap's account of what makes verification more or less complete. According to Carnap, this is a question of considering observation-statements which are inferred from the statement to be verified; and our verification will be more or less complete according as we check out a greater or smaller number of such observation-statements. But the fact of being inferred from the statement to be verified may be quite irrelevant. From the statement 'All men wear ties' we may infer that John Smith wears a tie. Yet an observation to this effect would not in the least serve to confirm the statement that all men wear ties. On the other hand, one can sometimes verify a statement by means of a single observation which is not inferable from it, or is so only in some weak sense of 'infer'. One may, for example, verify that there has been an earthquake somewhere by reading about it in the newspaper. But what makes this a method of verification is not that, given the statement, one could have predicted its publication in the newspaper; one may, on the contrary, be surprised to find it there.[18] Verification, and completeness of verification, are not matters that can be accounted for abstractly in terms of numbers and inference-relations.

A similar point may be made about the programme of analysis discussed in section 4.1. We saw there that there is no strict entailment from statements about tables and chairs to the relevant observation-statements. But it would be wrong to conclude that there is *no* entailment. If there is a table in my study, then it follows that if you go into my study, you will see a table. It does not follow in strict logic, but nevertheless it follows. It is true that all sorts of conditions (an indefinite set) are here taken for granted — that there is light, that you have normal eyes and are not distracted by something else, that the table is of a normal size and not hidden, and so on; but normally they are taken for

---

[18] Compare Wittgenstein's remark, quoted page 25.

granted. And normally (though not strictly) you would be contradicting the statement about the table if you said you hadn't seen one. Conversely, if you said you had seen one, then it would follow – in a suitable sense of 'follow' – that there is a table there. (In this case one of the conditions taken for granted would be that you intend to speak the truth.) These remarks apply to ordinary tables in ordinary rooms, but not for other sorts of objects in other sorts of circumstances. There is no single formula for describing the relations between a statement and the relevant observations.

4.5 THE PAST AND THE FUTURE

I can verify that there is a table in the study by going to have a look. By putting my hand out of the window I can verify that it is raining. In the case of such statements there is an obvious connection between meaning and method of verification. Part, at least, of what one is saying in making these statements is that, as Schlick put it, 'under these particular circumstances this particular experience will occur' (quoted page 57). But how would this work with statements about what was or what will be? It was sometimes thought that these must be analysed into experiences had, or to be had, at the present time. In his 'Meaning and Verification' of 1936, Schlick considered the view that statements about the future 'did not really refer to the future at all but asserted only the present existence of certain expectations' – a view which, he thought, could be found in Carnap's *Logischer Aufbau der Welt*. But, he continued,

> our definition of meaning does not imply such absurd consequences, and when someone asked, 'But how can you verify a proposition about a future event?', we replied, 'Why, for instance, by waiting for it to happen! "Waiting" is a perfectly legitimate method of verification'. (*GA* p. 345, *PP* p. 462.)

But obviously this is not a method that could be used for statements about the past. Such statements were considered by Waismann in his post-verificationist *Principles of Linguistic Philosophy*. He took as an example the statement 'It rained yesterday'.

> If I were asked how it could be verified, I should perhaps in the first moment be at a loss and then make various suggestions. I could ask other persons, or look up the meteorological report of the previous day, I could examine the traces of moisture on the ground, or resort to my own memory.

Yet, he said, the statement 'It rained yesterday' obviously does not mean any of these things. 'It seems,' he concluded, 'that the meaning of a sentence has nothing whatsoever to do with its verification' (*PLP* p. 329, *ER* p. 51).

This is going too far. The method of verification of Waismann's statement does have something to do with its meaning; and by his reaction to the question 'how it could be verified' he shows his understanding of its meaning.[19] But it is true that the connection is less definite and that there seems to be an obvious discrepancy between meaning and method of verification. As Waismann put it, the latter is 'irregular, loose, fluctuating, while the sentence always means the same' (*PLP* p. 330, *ER* p. 52).

There is, however, another way of relating these statements to methods of verification. This way was taken by Ayer in his 1946 preface to *Language, Truth and Logic*. Here he rejected the view that statements about the past 'can somehow be translated into propositions about present or future experiences'. This rejection did not mean, however, that these statements 'cannot be analysed in phenomenal terms; for they can be taken as implying that certain observations would have occurred if certain conditions had been fulfilled' (*LTL* pp. 24–5). We have already seen that the phenomenalist analysis relies largely on hypothetical statements about what *would* be experienced in suitable circumstances. Here we have what seems a natural extension, to

---

[19]Compare Wittgenstein's discussion of the verification of 'Julius Caesar crossed the Alps', *PB* pp. 86–7.

statements about what *would have been* experienced, 'if certain conditions had been fulfilled'.

A drawback of this view compared with the former is that it may make statements about the past appear unverifiable. As Ayer admitted, 'these conditions never can be fulfilled; for they require of the observer that he should occupy a temporal position that *ex hypothesi* he does not'. But Ayer saw no special difficulty here. It was, he argued,

> not a peculiarity of propositions about the past, for it is true also of unfilfilled conditions about the present that their protases cannot in fact be satisfied, since they require of the observer that he should be occupying a different spatial position from that which he actually does. (*LTL* p. 25.)

But this answer is unlikely to allay the objector's worry. For he may point out that whereas one can *change* one's 'spatial position' (to make the required observations), one cannot change one's 'temporal position'. (He may add that the very notion of a position is spatial and not temporal.)

In a later writing Ayer argued that there is no special problem about the past, because the tense of a statement is not really part of its meaning. Here he distinguished meaning or 'factual content' from the 'indication' given by the use of a particular tense. Thus

> there is no difference in meaning between the statements 'George VI was crowned in 1937', 'George VI is being crowned in 1937', and 'George VI will be crowned in 1937'. They differ in the indications that they respectively give of the temporal point of view from which they are made, but not, I think, in their factual content.[20]

Ayer thought that this would enable him to deal with the question of verifiability. Since the pastness of a statement was not part of its meaning, it would not matter that it was

---

[20] 'Statements about the Past', in *Philosophical Essays*, p. 186. For further discussion of this essay, see Bernard Williams and A. J. Ayer in *Perception and Identity*, ed. G. F. Macdonald, pp. 252ff. and 325ff.

unverifiable by the person making it. 'It may be required of [such statements] that they be verifiable, but not that they be verifiable by this or that particular person' (*Philosophical Essays* pp 188–9). But, it may be asked, what right has Ayer to disallow the tense of a statement from being part of its factual content? The fact that George VI's coronation lies in the past is, it may be said, no less a fact, albeit a special sort of fact, than other facts about his coronation. And Ayer may be accused of excluding it merely because it conflicts with his ideas about meaning and verification.

But there is no need for such drastic surgery in order to save the idea of phenomenalist analysis. As we saw in sections 4.1 and 4.3, that analysis depends to a large extent on unfulfilled hypotheticals; this being true of statements in the present no less than those in the past tense. Thus the meaning of 'George VI is being crowned' will consist to a large extent of unfulfilled hypotheticals. It is true that the analysis of statements about the past will always be different from that of statements about the present; and that there is a sort of direct verification that is possible for the latter but not for the former. But this need not be regarded as a difficulty for the phenomenalist—verificationist view. On the contrary, it may be said that the difference of verification-conditions is a true reflection of the difference in meanings.

Another sort of difficulty was raised by Bertrand Russell in his essay 'Logical Positivism'. The statement 'There was once a world without life' cannot, he said, mean that 'if I had been alive then, I should have seen that nothing was alive'.[21] But the verificationist does not have to express himself in this paradoxical way. He may speak of 'nothing else' rather than 'nothing'. This is, indeed, a normal way of understanding the word 'nothing' in such contexts. A space-traveller exploring the moon would not be contradicting himself if he reported that nothing was alive; neither would someone who describes the room in which he is standing as empty.[22]

[21] Bertrand Russell, *Logic and Knowledge,* ed. R. C. Marsh, p. 374.

[22] Schlick discussed the statement 'If all minds should disappear from the universe, the stars would still go on in their courses' in 'Meaning and Verification', *GA* p. 366, *PP* pp. 479–80. For Carnap's treatment of the same example, see *TM* p. 88.

Our discussion so far may give the impression that there is a neat correlation between the tense of a statement and the way in which it is related to its method of verification. But this would be a mistake. Consider once more the statement that there is a table in the study, and compare it with 'There will be a table in the study in two minutes'. Suppose now that it takes me two minutes to get to the study: which of these statements will I have verified when I see the table? Perhaps it will be said that, strictly speaking, it is the one that was made in the future tense; that I could not, strictly speaking, verify a statement in the present tense except by an observation made at the time of utterance. But this would be at odds with normal uses of 'verify'. We normally speak of verification as putting an end to uncertainty. Informed that there is a table in the study, but not being certain that this is so, I can go and verify it by making the necessary observation. But if someone says 'Here is a table' when I have the table in full view, then there is no information and no uncertainty; and it would be odd to say that I have verified a statement. It is also possible for the verification of a present-tense statement to have taken place in the past. Someone who saw the table there two minutes ago may be said to have verified the statement, made now, that there is a table there. A guide-book informs me of how things *are*. What it says *was* verified by the publishers last year and *will be* verified by me when I visit the places mentioned. What the guide-book says, and what I shall be verifying, is not that the church will have a Norman font, but that it has one; and what the publishers verified is not that it had a Norman font, but that it has one.

But these remarks, again, are not deduced from any formal logical schema; they presuppose background knowledge of the type of object and the circumstances. The remarks about the table, for example, will not be correct if we are talking about tables which are frequently being moved (card-tables, perhaps). And what is true for Norman fonts will not be true for less durable objects.

4.6 THE LANGUAGE OF SCIENCE

There are, as we have seen, various logical difficulties about verification. But sometimes verification is difficult, or even impossible, for technical reasons. Consider, for example, statements about the far side of the moon. When Schlick and Ayer considered this example, verification was impossible. But it would seem absurd to say that such statements suddenly became meaningful with the advent of space-travel. Ayer dealt with this case by a natural extension of the use of hypotheticals. No rocket had yet been invented, he said, to enable him to verify a statement about the far side of the moon; 'but I know what observations would decide it for me, if, as is theoretically conceivable, I were once in a position to make them'. Such statements were, he said, 'verifiable in principle' (*LTL* pp. 48–9).

It may be doubted, however, whether this phrase, and the phrase 'theoretically conceivable', are suitable for Ayer's purpose. For there are other statements, about more distant parts of the universe, say, whose verification is, according to accepted theories and principles of science, impossible. This was recognized by Schlick when he claimed that 'even if it could be shown that a journey to another celestial body were absolutely incompatible with the known laws of nature, a proposition about the other side of the moon would still be meaningful' (*GA* pp. 352–3, *PP* p. 468). All that was required, he said, was the 'logical possibility' of verification (*GA* p. 348, *PP* p. 464). This would be enough to enable us to say that such and such observations, though impossible, would have served to verify the statement. In the case of metaphysics, by contrast, we would not be able to describe such observations. Carnap, in a further discussion, distinguished between 'testability' – where a method of confirming or disconfirming a statement is available, and 'confirmability' – where this is not so, but 'we know that our observation of such and such a course of events would confirm the sentence' (*TM* p. 47).

There is, however, another kind of difficulty of verification which needs to be considered. A layman, faced with a scientific statement, may have no idea of its method of verification, actual or hypothetical. In section 2.3 I drew a distinction between 'essential' and 'non-essential' methods of verification — those that are, and those that are not, essential to an ordinary person's understanding of a statement. Among the latter were scientific methods, such as barometer readings, ignorance of which would not disqualify one from understanding such a statement as 'It is raining'. But what are we to say about the understanding of scientific statements having only scientific methods of verification?

> Let us imagine that wave-mechanics is explained in a lecture. How can we ascertain whether a listener has understood the meaning of this theory? Is it sufficient that he can repeat it in his own words? Or that he has vivid images? Or that he can draw normal conclusions? All this would not prove to us that he has really understood the meaning. There is only one method which we must adopt in order to find the answer: we must ask him how he would set about investigating the truth of this theory . . . If . . . he can state some experiment which confirms or refutes the propositions of wave-mechanics, then he has understood the theory. (*PLP* p. 325.)

We can readily agree with Waismann that knowing the method of verification is an important criterion of understanding the theory. But can there be *no* understanding of it without that? If the man can 'repeat it in his own words' and 'draw normal conclusions' from it, then he understands it at least to some extent. On the other hand, if he could 'state some experiments' but could not satisfy the previous conditions, then his understanding of it would not be complete either.

Consider the statement that the temperature at the centre of the sun is 13 million °C. I have no idea how this could be verified. The same is true of the statements that a fly's wings vibrate at the rate of so many beats per second, and that air is composed (let us say) of three gases. There is more to this difficulty than mere ignorance, such as could be remedied by asking an expert or consulting a book. For a layman, on being told the answer (how the statements are to be verified), may be unable to understand it or the concepts in which it is framed. They may be meaningless to him. Must we conclude that the statements, likewise, are meaningless to him? What we may say, and indeed should say, is that they do not mean *the same* to him as to the expert; and that this is so, at least partly, because of the latter's understanding of methods of verification.

The layman would be able to explain what the statements mean to him, and to show that they mean something to him, in spite of his ignorance of methods of verification. He can refer to the words used, such as 'temperature' and 'the sun', and show that he knows their meanings (and the relevant methods of verification) in contexts in which he is at home. It is true that knowing the meaning of a word in familiar contexts is not enough to guarantee knowledge of its meaning elsewhere. It may indeed not have any meaning there. But, assuming that it does, and supposing that the layman has explained his understanding in the way I have described, it would be wrong to deny that he has *any* understanding of the scientific statement.

So much for the discrepancy between meaning and verification due to the ignorance of the layman. Another sort of difficulty arises where the method of verification is known, but appears to fall short of what the statement is saying. The statement that the universe is expanding, for example, is verified by the observation that the light emitted from remote galaxies is redder than would otherwise be expected (the 'red shift'). Yet the statement does not seem to be merely about red shifts. Should a verificationist maintain that the statement (that the universe is expanding) is 'in principle' verifiable more directly, in the same sort of way as ordinary statements about expanding (or receding) objects? It is not clear what this would mean in the case of such a statement. The alternative is to insist that the statement does not, after all, mean anything beyond the known and describable methods of verification. This was the view taken by Schlick, who regarded it as merely another application of the verification principle. That principle, he thought, had been vindicated by 'Einstein's answer to the question, What do we mean when we speak of two events at distant places happening simultaneously?'

This answer consisted in a description of an experimental method by which the simultaneity of such events was actually ascertained. Einstein's philosophical opponents maintained — and some of them still maintain — that they knew the meaning of the above question independently of any method of verification . . . (*G4* p 341, *PP* p 459)

An opponent of Schlick's view would not, however, need to say that he 'knew the meaning of the above question' — whether two events are simultaneous — 'independently of any method of verification'. His point may be, rather, that the meaning of Einstein's talk of simultaneity is not exhausted by the 'description of an experimental method', as Schlick claims. And he may say, similarly, that the statement about the expanding universe means more than a description of the method of observing red shifts and the like. In support of this view he may argue that there would be no contradiction in supposing that all the observations are positive and yet the universe is not expanding.

Schlick, as I said, regarded 'Einstein's answer' to the question about simultaneity as a vindication of the verification principle. He seems not to have noticed that the use of such words as 'simultaneous' and 'expand' in scientific contexts poses a special problem for the principle. The 'experimental method' appropriate to Einstein's question will obviously be very different from the verification of ordinary statements about simultaneous events — for example, that the rainbow happened at the same time as the cuckoo's song. If meaning is to be identified with method of verification, then the meaning of the word in one context must be very different from its meaning in the other. How then does it come about that the same word is used in both?

In his paper Schlick referred with approval to P. W. Bridgman, who had introduced 'operationism' into the philosophy of science. Using the concept of length as an example, Bridgman had written:

. . . the concept of length involves as much and nothing more than the set of operations by which length is determined. In general, we mean by any concept nothing more

than a set of operations; *the concept is synonymous with
the corresponding set of operations.*[23]

In another passage Bridgman had faced the problem about
using the same word in statements with different methods
('operations') of verification.

> Strictly speaking, length when measured . . . by light
> beams should be called by another name, since the opera-
> tions are different.
> . . . in the extension from terrestrial to greater stellar dis-
> tances the concept of length has changed completely in
> character. To say that a certain star is 105 light years dis-
> tant is actually and conceptually an entirely different *kind*
> of thing from saying that a certain goal post is 100 meters
> distant.[24]

Bridgman tried to explain the use of the same word in
both cases by speaking of intermediate cases, where the
methods appropriate for stars and for football fields might
both be applied. But if this is right, then why should he insist
that distance in the case of stars 'is actually and conceptually
an entirely different *kind* of thing' from what it is in ordinary
statements? The only motive for saying this is the determina-
tion to identify meaning with method of verification. But an
astronomer would hardly wish to admit that when he uses
the word 'distance', he is not really talking about distance.
And if it is pointed out that his statements are not verifiable
in the same way as ordinary statements about distance, he
may answer that this is only a problem if one accepts the
verificationist-operationist view of meaning.

Perhaps the verificationist should accept that his principle
cannot be straightforwardly applied to such cases. He may
still hope to show that the astronomer's use of the concept is

[23] Bridgman, *The Logic of Modern Physics,* p. 3.

[24] *The Logic of Modern Physics,* pp. 8–9. A similar point was made by Wittgenstein, as recorded in *WWK* p. 204, in regard to the bisection of an angle. This, he
said, has 'an entirely different sense', according to whether the verification is by
measuring or by proof from axioms of geometry. (In this example, however, the
difference between the two methods of verification is of a different order.)

grounded, via intermediate cases, on methods of verification appropriate to ordinary uses.

The problem just discussed arises from the use of ordinary words in scientific contexts. But scientists also make use of technical terms; and here operationism may seem to be a promising approach. Such concepts as 'neutron' and 'quasar' are not rooted in ordinary language as are the concepts of distance and simultaneity. There are no ordinary uses, or ordinary methods of verification, for them. Such concepts, it was thought, can only be understood in terms of the technical operations required for their verification. But again, though it is true that this is an important aspect of understanding, it is not the whole story. Such concepts have their place within a theory and cannot be properly understood in isolation from the theory. The relevant experiments confirm the theory, and not merely the statements containing these concepts.[25]

Perhaps it will be thought that the operationist approach could be applied to the whole theory. On this view the theory would mean nothing more than the set of operations required to verify it. But if this were so, then it should be possible to construct only *one* theory from a given set of operations. The fact that, on the contrary, different theories are put forward on the same data, shows that there is more than that to the meaning of a theory.

As an extreme illustration of this point, we may take a theory from which no observations are deducible. Such a theory should be meaningless on the verificationist view. An example was considered by J. O. Wisdom in his 'Metamorphoses of the Verifiability Theory of Meaning' (*Mind,* 1963). Wisdom pointed out that when Einstein's General Theory of Relativity was announced in 1915, only one observable consequence (concerning the motion of Mercury) was thought to be deducible from it. And 'if there had been no such planet, or if Mercury had not been so close to the sun, this test

---

[25] See e.g. Paul Henle in Schilpp (ed.) *The Philosophy of Rudolf Carnap,* especially pp. 178–80; also C. G. Hempel, 'A Logical Appraisal of Operationism', in *Aspects of Scientific Explanation;* and R. B. Braithwaite, *Scientific Explanation,* ch. 3. A proper discussion of scientific concepts would be beyond the scope of this book.

would not have existed' (p. 338). The deduction of consequences, and the devising of techniques for making the observations, may themselves be major developments occurring
years after a theory is propounded. Moreover, no one can
know at that time whether they would ever take place. It
would seem to follow, on the verificationist view, that no
one would know what the theory meant or whether it had
any meaning at all. Furthermore, this question itself might
never be answered; for even if no observable consequences
were ever deduced, it would still remain conceivable that
some might be.

In this section I have discussed a number of problems
about the meaning and verification of scientific statements.
The subject is an extensive one, and to explore it fully would
be beyond the scope of this book. But enough has been said
to show that there is no single account of the relation of
meaning and verification which will be true both for ordinary
language and for the statements of science. There is also a
variety of situations in the case of the latter. But these difficulties do not mean that there is *no* truth in the verification
principle when applied to scientific theories. There is still a
connection between understanding such a theory – or understanding it fully – and being clear about the method of verification.[26] But being clear about the method of verification is
not simply a matter of knowing that such and such observations will be made if these and these experiments are set up.
It is also a matter of understanding what verification means
in relation to a given theory or scientific statement, and to
what extent, and in which situations, it plays a part in understanding. A further point here is that scientific theories are
not 'verified' or 'true' in the same sense as ordinary statements. There is a table in the study; this is true and I have
verified it. But when we turn to scientific theories, we may
hesitate to speak of truth or verification at all. In the case of
Einstein's theory or, say, Darwin's theory of the origin of

[26] Although Wittgenstein had little time for verificationism by the time he came
to write the *Investigations*, he continued to see a connection between verification
and understanding. 'Asking whether and how a proposition can be verified is only
a particular way of asking "How d'you mean?" The answer is a contribution to
the grammar of the proposition' (*PI* 353).

species, we may prefer to speak of a 'good' or 'satisfactory' theory, or one that is (or is not) 'well confirmed'. This is not because our knowledge here is necessarily less secure, in the sense in which, say, I may be not quite certain whether there is a table in the other room. It is because of differences in the ways in which verification is relevant in different types of discourse.

5 The Elimination of Experience

5.1 THE 'FORMAL MODE' OF SPEECH

At the start of the last chapter we saw how the verification of an ordinary statement was to consist of two stages, corresponding to the words 'Logical Empiricism'. The statement would be analysed by a logical process into 'elementary' statements, and then would come the crucial contact with experience, as required by empiricism. Waismann evidently regarded the second stage as the real verification, the first being merely a means to it. 'To analyse a proposition means to consider how it is to be verified. Language *touches* reality with elementary propositions . . . What elementary propositions describe are: phenomena (experiences).'[1]

What must be our surprise, then, when we read in the writings of a leading verificationist that analysis is the whole of verification, and that the crucial appeal to experience falls away. 'In all empirical sciences', wrote Carnap, 'Logical Analysis involves the problem of verification'; but this, he went on, only concerns 'the logical inferential relations between statements in general and so-called protocol or observation statements' (*US* p. 25). What happens, then, about verification of the latter? Is it not here that we must pass from analysis to experience? This seems to be the view taken a few pages later, where we read that these statements 'refer to the given, and describe directly given experience or phenomena, i.e. the simplest states of which knowledge can be had' (p. 45). It turns out, however, that this account is regarded by Carnap as not quite satisfactory; being expressed, as he puts it, in the 'material' as opposed to the 'formal' mode of speech.

[1] *WWK* p. 249.

77

By the material mode Carnap meant any kind of speech in which there is reference to facts, objects or phenomena, as opposed to words; the formal mode, on the other hand, 'refers only to linguistic forms' (*US* p. 38). In the material mode we may say, for example, that economics is about phenomena such as supply and demand; translated into the formal mode, this becomes a statement about the words used in economics: 'its sentences can be constructed from the expressions "supply and demand" . . . etc., put together in such and such a way' (p. 41).

The shift to the formal mode was regarded by Carnap and his followers as being of the greatest importance to philosophy. It was thought that if only philosophers would express themselves in the formal mode, most of the traditional problems and obscurities could not arise. In his *Logical Syntax of Language* Carnap gave various illustrations of the advantages of the formal mode as he saw them. He imagined a philosopher, engaged in discussion about the concept of number, making the statement 'Five is not a thing but a number'. This sentence, he claimed, has a misleading resemblance to one which 'expresses a property of the number five, like the sentence "Five is not an even but an odd number"'. But, said Carnap, the former sentence was not really 'concerned with the number five, but with the word "five"'. Hence it would be better to express it in the formal mode, thus: ' "Five" is not a thing-word but a number-word' (*LSL* p. 285). By treating the claim as a claim about words, confusion and useless controversy would be avoided.

Now as we saw above, Carnap had spoken — using the material mode — of observation-statements as being about 'experience or phenomena, i.e. the simplest states of which knowledge can be had'. When we read his translation of this into the formal mode, we find a remarkable transformation. Gone are the references to experience and phenomena (these being items other than words). Instead of characterizing the basic statements in these terms, we are to say merely that they are 'statements needing no justification and serving as

[2] The German *Bewährung* could be translated as 'verification' rather than 'justification'.

the foundation for all the remaining statements of science' (*US* p. 45).[2] In another passage Carnap recommended that 'instead of speaking of the "content of experience", "sensations of colour" and the like, we [should] refer to "protocol statements" or "protocol statements involving names of colours" ' (p. 83).

Thus the crucial contact with experience is broken. The demands of empiricism are to be met by tracing logical relations between statements, and nothing more. Any reference to experience will be a confusion due to use of the material mode. What led Carnap to this drastic step? On the ordinary empiricist view, meaning is based on experience; what a person means by a given expression is, or is determined by, certain experiences that he has. But this, argued Carnap, entails that the meaning of the expression is peculiar to that person. Thus the sentence 'I am thirsty', 'though composed of the same sounds, would have different senses when uttered by S_1 and S_2 respectively . . . No statement in S_2's protocol language can express the thirst of S_1. For all such statements express only what is immediately given to S_2'. (*US* pp. 78–9.)

Carnap also maintained, however, that when we speak of physical objects our language is 'intersubjective'; that in this case the sounds used by different speakers do have the same meaning. But what could be the connection between the intersubjective 'physical' language and the plurality of subjective 'protocol languages'? Must we not conclude that 'physical statements . . . float in a void disconnected, in principle, from all experience'? (*US* p. 81). There was, thought Carnap, a ready way of avoiding such intractable questions. 'These pseudo-questions', he wrote, 'are automatically eliminated by using the formal mode' (p. 83). If we confine ourselves to statements about language, then we shall say merely that these and these expressions are used, and that they occupy such and such a logical place in the system – for example that of 'needing no justification and serving as the foundation for all the remaining statements of science'. In this way we would be speaking throughout about intersubjective items and relations, so that problems about the subjectivity of experience could not arise.

5.2 PROTOCOL STATEMENTS

On the view represented by the 'material' mode, the basic
statements are characterized by their content: they 'describe
directly given experience or phenomena'. In the formal
mode, as we have just seen, they are characterized by their
logical place in the system. But a number of questions arise
about these statements. How may we recognize them? Why
do they need 'no justification'?

Carnap confessed himself undecided about the form that
the protocol statements should take. They might, he thought,
consist of such expressions as 'Joy now' and 'Here now blue';
or they might be about 'entire sensory fields'; or again, they
might be more like ordinary sentences, such as 'A red cube is
on the table' (*US* pp. 46–7). There are various difficulties
about these forms of words. But a general objection, made by
Otto Neurath, was that none of them could be fitted into the
intersubjective system of science unless the reference of
'now' and 'here', and the identity of the speaker, were
known.[3] To show what was required of a protocol statement,
this knowledge must be made explicit. He gave the following
as a suitable example: 'Otto's protocol at 3:17 o'clock: [At
3:16 o'clock Otto said to himself: (at 3:15 o'clock there was
a table in the room perceived by Otto)]' (*ER,* p. 163).

This example will not do as it stands, because terms like
'Otto', '3:17' and 'the room' are still not intersubjective in
the required sense. We who read the statement today, for
example, would not know where in the system to place the
two latter terms; and if we know who Otto was, we do not
know it from the statement alone. Perhaps Neurath thought
of his example as indicating the way towards a more complex
statement which would achieve what was required.

We can recognize Neurath's example as a protocol statement, because the term 'protocol' is used in it. But is the

---

[3] 'Protokollsätze', *Erkenntnis* 1923–3. This paper is translated, under the title
'Protocol Sentences', in *LP* and *ER*. Neurath regarded as 'metaphysical' the
references to facts in Wittgenstein's *Tractatus*. 'That a fact should be reflected in
the structure of a statement was for him pure metaphysics' (M. Neurath and R. S.
Cohen, eds., *Otto Neurath: Empiricism and Sociology,* p. 47). Compare note 6,
page 4 above.

statement entitled to this designation? It does not enjoy the
special status of experiential statements in the first person,
on account of which these had been regarded as protocol
statements providing the foundation of science. The traditional view had been that these statements enjoy a special
kind of certainty and thus provide the foundation of all
knowledge.[4] This status is not possessed by statements in the
third person, such as those about Otto's thoughts or observations. Neurath recognized this, and denied that there were
any statements having the special status. 'No sentence,' he
declared, 'enjoys the "Noli me tangere" which Carnap ordains
for protocol sentences' (*ER* pp. 164–5). To illustrate the
point he asked the reader to imagine an ambidextrous person
writing down two contradictory protocols at the same time.

Neurath's arguments are a reasonable development of
Carnap's quest for intersubjectivity. But what is the point
now of speaking of protocol statements at all? We should
not, Carnap has told us, refer to them as statements that
'describe directly given experience', for that would be going
outside the formal mode. Nor can we, as Neurath has shown,
regard them as distinguished by a special kind of certainty.
What then is left of the notion of protocol statements? There
is, remarked Ayer, 'no more justification for it than there
would be for making a collection of all the propositions that
could be correctly expressed in English by sentences beginning with the letter B, and choosing to call them Basic propositions'.[5]

It is not hard to see why Carnap and his colleagues were
reluctant to give up the idea of protocol statements. They
wanted to regard science, reasonably enough, as based on
experiment and observation. 'Science is a system of statements based on direct experience, and controlled by experimental verification ... Verification is based upon "protocol
statements" ...' Thus wrote Carnap (albeit in the material
mode) in the opening pages of his monograph. But as Ayer
observed, 'one does not become an empiricist merely by a

[4]Such a view had been expressed by Ayer, as quoted on pages 39–40.

[5]'Verification and Experience', *LP* p. 231.

free use of the word "empirical" or the word "observation" '
(*FEK* p. 90).

The occurrence of the word 'protocol' in Neurath's
example is similarly misleading since it cannot have any bearing on the status of the example. If, while out for a walk, I
came across a piece of paper bearing the sentence S, I might
or might not believe what it says. But it would not help me
to decide the question if the paper were headed 'Otto's protocol' — unless I already had some relevant knowledge of
Otto and Otto's habits. (This knowledge could, of course,
affect the question either way.) Similarly, I might have
reason to think that S is more likely to be true (or false) if
the paper were placed in a cardboard box; but this would not
show anything of general interest about statements presented
in this way.

In later writings Carnap regarded the question which statements should serve as protocols as 'a matter of decision'. It
did not matter, he said, which statements were chosen. 'One
can always go beyond any given statement; *there are no
absolute starting-points* for the construction of science.' He
admitted that 'in practical matters' one would often regard
one's own observation-statements as final. 'But', he said, 'this
is of no significance in principle. It only happens because the
intersubjective testing of statements about observations
(brain-processes) is relatively inconvenient and difficult'.[6]
Carnap believed that statements about observations and experiences were translatable into statements about brain processes; they were thus intersubjective, no less than other
statements about the physical world. (These views will be
further discussed in section 6.2.)

5.3 THE COHERENCE THEORY AND THE 'WARNING OF A TRUE EMPIRICIST'

After the elimination of experience, what becomes of verification and truth? The whole weight must now be borne by
the logical relations between statements. Neurath proposed
that we might think of the system of science as a sort of

[6]'Über Protokollsätze', *Erkenntnis* (1932–33), pp. 224–6.

'sorting-machine, into which the protocol sentences are thrown'.

> The laws and other factual sentences (including protocol sentences) serving to mesh the machine's gears sort the protocol sentences which are thrown into the machine and cause a bell to ring if a contradiction ensues. At this point one must either replace the protocol sentence whose introduction into the machine has led to the contradiction by some other protocol sentence, or rebuild the entire machine. *Who* rebuilds the machine, or *whose* protocol sentences are thrown into the machine, is of no consequence whatsoever (*ER* p. 168).

The Carnap–Neurath account is usually described as a version of the 'coherence theory' of truth, according to which the truth of a statement is a matter of its coherence with other statements.[7] It appears, however, that the account before us amounts to a theory of falsehood rather than truth; for it tells us what to do if the bell rings but not if it is silent. The statements 'There is life on other planets' and 'Caesar scratched his head while crossing the Rubicon' would not, presumably, cause Neurath's bell to ring, not being in contradiction with existing knowledge. Should we therefore accept them as true? Ordinarily we might say of such statements that they cannot be true unless they cohere with what we know already — but that we cannot tell whether they *are* true unless we could make suitable observations. But the latter criterion is now excluded.

Supposing, however, that the bell does ring: how shall we decide which statements to retain and which to reject? We cannot ascribe a favoured status to those already in the machine (any more than to those bearing the label 'protocol'); for to do so would be to appeal to a criterion other than coherence. Neurath tells us that when the bell rings we may either replace the new statement or reconstruct the

---

[7] It is a matter of some irony that the coherence theory had previously been represented by such non-empiricist thinkers as Bradley and Joachim. See F. H. Bradley, *Appearance and Reality* and H. Joachim, *The Nature of Truth*.

machine. But which of these courses should we take in a given case? And if different options are taken by different individuals or groups, what grounds could there be for regarding any one of them, rather than another, as representing the truth?

The coherence theory has not been short of critics. Prominent among them was the leader of the Vienna Circle. 'Anyone', wrote Schlick,

> who takes coherence seriously as the sole criterion of truth . . . must consider any fabricated tale to be no less true than a historical report . . . so long as the tale is well enough fashioned to harbour no contradictions anywhere. With the aid of fantasy I can portray a grotesque world of adventure; the coherence philosopher has to believe in the truth of my account, provided only that I have a care for the mutual consistency of my claims and discreetly avoid any collision with the customary description of the world, by laying the scene of my recital on a distant star, where observation is no longer possible. Indeed, strictly speaking, I have no need at all of such discretion; I can equally insist that others have to adjust themselves to my story, and not the other way round. The others cannot even object, in that case, that this procedure conflicts with observation . . .[8]

In a subsequent paper Schlick described his remarks as 'nothing but a gentle warning of a true empiricist' against what seemed to him 'a rather dogmatic or rationalistic formulation of positivistic principles'.[9] A series of attacks and counter-attacks on the subject of Schlick's 'gentle warning' now appeared in the pages of *Erkenntnis* and those of the recently founded British journal, *Analysis.* One of those who took up Schlick's challenge was Carl Hempel, who considered the question how we are 'to distinguish the true protocol statements of science from the false ones of a fairy tale'.

[8] 'On the Foundation of Knowledge', *GA* p. 297, *PP* p. 376, *ER* pp. 184–5.
[9] 'Facts and Propositions', *Analysis* (1935), *PP* p. 400, *ER* p. 00.

As Carnap and Neurath emphasize, there is indeed no formal, no logical difference between the two compared systems, but an *empirical* one. The system of protocol statements which we call true . . . may be characterized by the historical fact that it is the system which is actually adopted by mankind, and especially by the scientists of our culture circle; and the 'true' statements in general may be characterized as those which are sufficiently supported by the system of actually adopted protocol statements.[10]

Hempel's response cannot be regarded as a direct answer to Schlick's problem. What Schlick wants to know is why, after the elimination of experience, we *should* adopt, or not adopt, a given system of beliefs. It is hardly an answer to this to say that a certain system *is* 'actually adopted' ('by mankind' or 'by the scientists of our culture circle', as the case may be). Hempel's point is, however, that Schlick's quest for justification is misguided; and that the answer he has given is the nearest that can be given to Schlick's question. It is an answer that does at least draw a distinction between the systems in question.

This distinction is, however, more precarious than it may at first appear. Hempel uses (and stresses) the word *'empirical'* to make the negative point that there is 'no formal, no logical difference between the two compared systems'. On his view our preference for one rather than the other is just a brute fact, like the fact that it is now raining. But the word 'empirical', as used by Hempel, cannot have the *positive* meaning that it normally has. In describing a statement as 'empirical', Hempel cannot be saying that it is to be verified by observation; for that would be going back to the old empiricist criterion of truth which the coherence theory was intended to supersede. The statement that this system is actually adopted can itself be subject, according to that theory, only to the test of coherence. If Schlick wanted his fairy tale to enjoy a similar distinction, he need only add to it a statement to the

---

[10]'On the Logical Positivists' Theory of Truth', *Analysis* (1935), p. 57. A similar line was taken by Carnap in his 'Reply to the foregoing papers by E. Zilsel and K. Duncker', *Erkenntnis* (1932–33).

same effect. And if this statement conflicts with the other, then again the question cannot be settled by observation.[11]

In evaluating Hempel's response to Schlick, it makes some difference whether we consider beliefs held 'by mankind' or 'by the scientists of our culture circle'. There are indeed facts about which no question can arise for normal human beings. If Schlick's fairy story went against these, then we can be sure that no one would actually claim to believe it. And then one sort of answer to the question 'What if someone said he believed . . .?', would be: 'We know that no one will'. But this answer will not do for beliefs that are, merely, outside the science of our culture circle. For we know very well that such beliefs are actually held, metaphysics and religion being two notable examples. We also know that conflicting beliefs are held among scientists and, again, that beliefs in other cultures differ from those of our own. In all these cases the claim of being 'actually adopted' confers no distinction, and we are left wih genuine problems about truth and falsity.

---

[11] Similar points were made by B. von Juhos, *Analysis* (1935), pp. 91–2; L. J. Russell, *Proceedings of the Aristotelian Society,* supp. vol. (1934), p. 191; and in *FEK* p. 92, *ER* pp. 172–3.

5.4 THE FORMAL MODE AND OSTENSIVE DEFINITION

The Logical Positivists, as has been pointed out, were especially concerned to give an empiricist account of meaning. What becomes of this after the change to the formal mode? The question of meaning was considered by Carnap in the opening pages of *The Unity of Science.* A language, he said there, consists of two elements, vocabulary and syntax. The syntax, he said, can be given in the form of rules; rules for forming words into sentences, and rules for transforming sentences into other sentences – either by way of inference or by way of translation. He then asked: 'But is it not also necessary, in order to understand the "sense" of sentences, to indicate the "meaning" of the words?' This question he answered firmly in the negative. 'No; the demand made thereby in the material mode is satisfied by specifying the formal rules which constitute [a word's] syntax' (*US* pp. 38–9).

But if the question of meaning is to be set aside in this way, are we still talking about language? Suppose that I and a number of friends make up a set of sounds ('words') which we form into patterns ('sentences') in accordance with certain rules, and with further rules prescribing the replacement ('translation') of some of these 'sentences' by others. This might produce some sort of party-game; but it would not amount to a language. It is true that sometimes a question about meaning can be answered by giving a replacement-rule. I may learn the meaning of sentence s by learning that it is replaceable by sentence t; or, say, by the conjunction t and u. But this is not a sufficient condition. For I may know that these sentences are replaceable by one another without knowing the meaning of any of them. They may, indeed, not have any meaning for all I know. For it might be that all of them are drawn from a system, like that imagined above, in which meaningless 'words' and 'sentences' are introduced together with a set of rules governing arrangement and replacement. Or perhaps they belong to a metaphysical system, which, though conforming to syntactical rules, is composed of 'pseudo-statements'.

Now as we saw in section 2.2, Schlick regarded ostensive definition as the key to the question of meaning. By its means, he thought, we escape from the circle of sentences defined by other sentences and make contact with the reality which gives meaning to the whole system. But Carnap recognized only the one kind of definition; a definition, he said, 'is a rule for the mutual transformation of words'. This, he went on,

is true both of so-called nominal [i.e. verbal] definitions (e.g. 'Elephant' = animal with such and such distinguishing characteristics) and also, a fact usually forgotten, for so-called ostensive definitions (e.g. 'Elephant' = animal of the same kind as the animal in this or that position in space-time).

'Both definitions', he concluded, 'are translations of words' (*US* p. 39).

It appears, however, that in the second case we do not

have a definition at all. In the first case, we might fill in 'such and such characteristics' by the phrase 'large pachyderm with proboscis and long ivory tusks'. This is a definition (or part of one) because the description is analytic to the concept 'elephant'; it is a matter of logic that it is true of elephants. But this is not so with descriptions of the second kind. As Ayer pointed out, it may be true that there was an elephant to be observed 30 yards south-west of the bandstand at the London Zoo on 2 July 1939, but it would not be necessarily true (*FEK* p. 89, *ER* p. 171). It is not analytic to the concept 'elephant' that such an animal was seen in that 'position in space-time'.

What Carnap has given us in the second case is not a verbal definition; but neither does it amount to an ostensive definition. If we fill in 'this or that position', for example in the way suggested by Ayer, we shall not necessarily get an ostensive definition. This will only be so if we add to Carnap's formula the stipulation that we are speaking to someone who was there at that time, looking at the animal. Alternatively (and this is what philosophers have usually had in mind) the definition would be given in the presence of the animal, using an expression such as 'Here is an elephant' or 'This is an elephant'; and this is even further removed from Carnap's formula. This kind of definition has interested philosophers just because, unlike a verbal definition, it cannot be described as 'a rule for the transformation of words'. In defining 'elephant' in this way, one is not relying merely on other words, but on the existence of a suitable situation.

It is doubtful whether a system in which there is no place for ostensive definition could be regarded as a language. For if there is no place for definitions of the form 'This is an elephant', then there cannot be any place for the corresponding questions either. Then we would not be able to ask 'What is this?' or 'Is this an elephant?', meaning the object before us.

It would seem, however, that these comparisons with what we know as language would not have impressed Carnap. For he came to see the task of the philosopher of language as one of invention rather than description. 'I came to recognize', he relates in the Schilpp volume, 'that our task is one of *plan-*

ning forms of languages'. This meant that one had to 'envisage the general structure of a system and to make, at different points in the system, a choice among various possibilities, theoretically an infinity of possibilities . . .'[12] In the *Logical Syntax of Language* he had introduced his 'Principle of Tolerance':

> Everyone is at liberty to build up his own logic, i.e. his own form of language, as he wishes. All that is required of him is that, if he wishes to discuss it, he must state his methods clearly, and give syntactical rules instead of philosophical arguments. (P. 52.)

It is difficult to know how literally to take these statements. As M. and W. C. Kneale have commented, in making up the rules of such a system 'we must use some language to formulate them, and reliance on this language inevitably carries with it acceptance of logical principles which are not established by convention alone'.[13] Moreover, when we read some of Carnap's actual remarks about language, for example (as mentioned on page 82) that observation-statements are translatable into statements about the brain, it is hardly possible to regard them as examples of 'building up one's own logic' (or 'form of language'). In saying that such a translation is possible Carnap is making a claim about the meanings of existing statements and not merely laying down rules for a system of his own invention.

5.5 'WHAT I SEE, I SEE!'; THE QUEST FOR FOUNDATIONS

There was no doubt in Schlick's mind as to the existence of a special class of statements in any system of knowledge. 'I would not', he declared,

---

[12] Schilpp (ed.), *The Philosophy of Rudolf Carnap*, p. 68.

[13] *The Development of Logic*, p. 635.

give up my own observation propositions under any circumstances, for I find, rather, that I can only adopt a
system of knowledge which they fit into without mutila-
tion . . . this support I would never allow to be taken from
me, my own observation propositions would always be the
final criterion. I would proclaim, as it were. What I see, I
see!' (*GA* p. 302, *PP* p. 380, *ER* pp. 188–9.)

In his robust defence of observation-statements, Schlick
seems to be speaking the language of common sense as
opposed to the paradoxical results of the coherence theory.
But as we follow him in his account of these statements, we
are taken rather a long way from ordinary ideas. Like Descartes, Schlick regarded it as essential to a system of knowledge that there must be a type of knowledge that is 'immune
from all doubt'; and he thought that this requirement was
fulfilled by observation-statements. He readily agreed, however, that these could not be the kind of observation-statements (protocol statements) described by Neurath, recording
an observation by a named person at such and such a time
and place. To be immune from doubt, the statement must be
confined strictly to what is observed at the time of making it,
and this would not include the observer's name, nor the
specifications of time and place. Only the words 'here' and
'now', insisted Schlick, would be admissible by way of
reference to time and place. He gave as examples 'Here now
two black spots coincide', 'Here now blue is bounded by
yellow' and 'Here now pain' (*GA* p. 308, *PP* p. 385, *ER*
p. 194). It will be noticed that these examples are similar to
those of Carnap, quoted on page 80, and rejected by Neurath.
Schlick also maintained, as did Neurath, that such statements
could not be fitted into the system of science like other statements. But this did not lead him to regard them as dispens-
able or unimportant.

He admitted, however, that they could not be regarded as
'foundations' of knowledge, for 'as soon as I put down the
demonstrative terms "here" and "now", they lose their
meaning' (*GA* p. 308, *PP* p. 386, *ER* p. 195). Schlick's point is
that the meanings of 'here' and 'now' are relative to the time
and place of utterance. A here-and-now statement that has

been made in the past cannot convey knowledge unless *other* knowledge, concerning the time and place of its utterance, is already in hand. Hence the here-and-now statement cannot be regarded as fundamental in the system of knowledge.

Another point concerns the meanings of words and statements generally. May not my statement, even if confined to the here and now, be wrong owing to a failure to remember the meanings of words correctly? In what sense, asked Schlick, 'can we speak of the "absolute certainty" of observation statements?' (*GA* p. 306, *PP* p. 383, *ER* p. 192.)

In dealing with these two points Schlick tried to bring out the special character and importance of observation-statements. In regard to the second point, he made a comparison with analytic statements. In the case of these, he claimed, knowledge of meaning is sufficient for knowledge of truth.

> For in an analytic judgement, to understand its meaning and to discern its *a priori* validity, are *one and the same process*. A synthetic statement, by contrast, is characterized by the fact that if I have merely discerned its meaning, I have no notion whether it is true or false . . . (*GA* p. 308, *PP* p. 385, *ER* p. 194.)

There is, continued Schlick, 'only one exception to this.' He was referring to the observation-statements; or, as he also called them, 'confirmations' (*Konstatierungen,* translated below as 'affirmations') – a term to be discussed shortly.

> Whereas in all other synthetic statements, establishing the meaning and establishing the truth are separate, clearly distinguishable processes, in observation statements they coincide, just as they do in analytic judgements. However different the 'affirmations' may be from analytic propositions, they have this in common, that in both the process of understanding is at the same time the process of verification. Along with their meaning I simultaneously grasp their truth. (*GA* p. 308, *PP* p. 385, *ER* p. 194.)

But what is meant here by 'grasping their meaning'? Schlick explained that when making such a statement, 'an experience occurs, the attention is directed to something observed'. But to grasp the meaning of a statement it is not enough to direct the attention to something (though this may help). Moreover, in ordinary cases of grasping a meaning we do not find the immunity from error that Schlick is after; for one may grasp a meaning wrongly. Presumably what Schlick had in mind was that one *gives* the statement its meaning, thereby *making* it mean that to which one is directing one's attention. That this is what he had in mind is indicated by his conflation elsewhere of ostensive definition and verification (discussed in section 2.2). The present case differs, however, from ordinary cases of ostensive definition, since there is no inter-personal transaction but only a private one. It is likely that Wittgenstein was thinking of Schlick when, in his later writings, he argued that the 'private ostensive definition' is no definition at all, and that an expression whose meaning is private in this sense is not a piece of language at all.[14]

It is in any case wrong to think that knowledge or 'absolute certainty' could be created by an act of definition. To know that *p* is to know something that is the case independently of one's act of defining 'p'; and one's statement that *p* is to be assessed (as true or false, knowledge or error) by reference to facts other than one's definition of 'p'. This is a general point, not confined to the kind of situation that Schlick attempted to describe. The same point may be made about a claim made recently by Saul Kripke, who takes for his example the standard metre in Paris.[15] It is, says Kripke, a contingent fact that the rod in Paris is one metre long; but what, he asks, 'is the *epistemological* status of the statement "Stick *S* is one metre long at t_0", for someone who has [at time t_0] fixed the metric system by reference to stick *S*? It would seem', says Kripke, 'that he knows it *a priori*'. 'In this sense', he concludes, 'there are contingent *a priori* truths'.

This claim about contingent *a priori* truths is comparable to what Schlick says, in the passages just quoted, about synthetic statements which are known in the same sort of way

---

[14] See e.g. *PI* 380 and 241 ff.

[15] 'Naming and Necessity', in Harman and Davidson (eds.), *Semantics of Natural Language*, p. 275.

as analytic ones. But again, it is wrong to represent someone who 'fixes the metric system' by reference to a standard rod as expressing *knowledge* of the length of the rod. His speech-act is not an expression of knowledge, but a prescription for the future use of a word.[16] Similarly, Schlick was mistaken if he thought that he could attain certainty by the expedient of making his statements mean the experiences to which he was directing his attention.

Let us turn to the other point, about the place of Schlick's observation-statements in the system of knowledge. As we saw, he argued that they cannot be regarded as fundamental, because of their restriction to the here and now. What then is their place in the system? That they must have a crucial place in it was evident, in Schlick's view, from their peculiar closeness to the source of all knowledge, experience itself.

> . . . everything here turns upon the character of immediacy which is peculiar to observation statements, and to which they owe their value both positive and negative; the positive value of absolute validity, and the negative value of being useless as an enduring foundation. (*GA* p. 309, *PP* pp. 385–6, *ER* pp. 194–5.)

Schlick's solution was to speak of these statements as 'confirmations' (*Konstatierungen*, translated below as 'affirmations') which, as he put it, come 'at the end' and not the beginning of knowledge. All other statements were to be regarded as 'hypotheses'; they were in a sense dependent on the fleeting 'confirmations', but not in the sense of being 'built up' from them.

> Upon affirmations no logically tenable structure can be erected, for they are already gone at the moment building begins. If they stand in time at the outset of the process of knowledge, they are logically of no use. It is quite other-wise, however, when they come at the end; they complete

---

[16] 'Naming and describing do not stand on the same level: naming is a preparation for description' (*PI* 49).

the act of verification (or falsification), and at the moment of their appearance have already performed their duty. (*GA* pp. 304–5, *PP* p. 382, *ER* p. 191.)

It is a puzzling feature of Schlick's 'confirmations' that he thinks of them sometimes as statements (in speaking of them as observation-statements) and sometimes as confirmatory experiences (as, apparently, in the passage just quoted).[17] This confusion was no accident. That which 'completes the act of verification' is not a statement but an observation; in this respect 'confirmation' must mean 'confirmatory experience'. That of which meaning and truth may be predicated, and of whose truth one may be absolutely certain, is the statement; in this respect 'confirmation' must mean the statement corresponding to the experience.

It is, according to Schlick, their peculiar closeness to experience that endows his observation-statements with absolute certainty. But it may be doubted whether these 'statements' are really statements at all; for a statement, in the ordinary sense, has a public and durable meaning, and this meaning is not bestowed on it by a speaker's act of directing his attention on something. Why did Schlick embark on his quest for statements which would be 'immune from all doubt'? He could have denied the coherence theory without producing such statements. If there are no such statements, it does not follow that truth is what the coherence theory says. In considering the meaning of 'true', we are not obliged to choose between 'coherent with other statements' and 'based on absolute certainties'. Indeed, neither of these definitions reflects the ordinary use of 'true'. On the other hand, if we reject the idea of absolute certainty, we may still argue that there is a kind of statements where doubt is essentially less likely; so that others can normally be checked against these. (Such a view is taken in courts of law.)

---

[17] In a subsequent paper in English he referred to 'those simple experiences which may be regarded as the final steps of a comparison between a statement and a fact and which I have spoken of as "Konstatierungen"'. ('Facts and Propositions', *Analysis*, 1935. *PP* p. 404, *ER* p. 201.)

But should we reject the idea of absolute certainty? Schlick's use of this expression is not the normal one. According to the normal use, it is quite often the case that one is absolutely certain of the truth of a statement – an ordinary statement, as opposed to the peculiar 'statements' introduced by Schlick. I am, for example, absolutely certain that Schlick was a member of the Vienna Circle, and it would be incorrect for me to deny that I am. What Schlick was seeking, however, was certainty in a rather special sense, a sense that he regarded as characteristic of analytic statements. He thought that his observation statements, though not analytic, enjoyed the same sort of certainty because of their special logical character. In this respect his enterprise was like that of Descartes, who ascribed a similar status to the statements 'I exist' and 'I am thinking'.

But Schlick's motive was not the same as Descartes's. He did not begin with a problem of scepticism which he tried to overcome by producing a piece of knowledge that is *a priori* and yet non-analytic. Schlick's motive was to vindicate empiricism. He believed that knowledge of empirical statements must be wholly reducible to corresponding experiences. This meant that there must be, somewhere in the system, statements whose meaning did not go beyond the speaker's experience at the time of speaking. But statements having this character, thought Schlick, must be more certain than any ordinary empirical statements could be. We may perhaps think of them as a sort of mirror-image accompanying the experience and faithfully reflecting it. But a mirror-image is not a statement.

5.6 COMMUNICABLE STRUCTURE AND INEFFABLE CONTENT

There was yet another way in which Schlick tried to explain the meaning of empirical statements. This was the account given in the lectures on 'Form and Content', delivered at the University of London in 1932 – perhaps the most subtle and

interesting of his writings.[18] This time the important relation
is not between experience and a special kind of statement, as
discussed in the last section. It is between ordinary statements and facts. And the relation in question is, according to
Schlick, one of identity of structure.

Both statements and facts have, according to Schlick, a
'logical structure'; and any given statement has (if true) the
same logical structure as the fact expressed by it. It is this
identity of structure that makes communication possible; and
when I communicate facts to you, 'my propositions express
these facts by conveying to you their logical structure' (*GA*
p. 160, *PP* p. 292, *ER* p. 134). He went on to speak of propositions themselves as 'facts'; so that 'we can say that we express a fact by another fact' (*GA* p. 171, *PP* p. 302, *ER* p.
144).[19]

Since the logical structures of facts and propositions
belong to them irrespective of speakers, we have here a way
in which language is intersubjective, unlike the 'confirmations' of the last section. But what happens now to the role
of the individual's experience, on which Schlick laid so much
emphasis? In the lectures Schlick spoke of this as 'content'.
He compared a blind man's use of a colour-word with that of
a sighted man. The former, he said, would be able to understand the word 'green' as something 'possessing a certain
structure or belonging to a certain system of internal relations'; hence the description of something as green would not
be meaningless to him. But Schlick went further and maintained that the description would mean just as much to the
blind as to the sighted man. For, he maintained, that which
makes the difference between the two men is not a matter
for description at all. Given that language 'can communicate
nothing but the logical structure of the green colour', it cannot communicate 'that ineffable quality of greenness which
appears to constitute its very nature . . . in short, its Content'

---

[18] Although they are earlier in date, I have found it convenient to discuss these
lectures after 'On the Foundation of Knowledge'.

[19] In the *Tractatus*, where propositions were regarded as a kind of picture, we
read: 'A picture is a fact' (2.141). There are many connections between Schlick's
account and that of the *Tractatus*, which I have not attempted to expound.

(*GA* p. 163, *PP* p. 295, *ER* p. 137). Content, he maintained, is subjective in a way that puts it beyond the reach of language.

> . . . every observer fills in his own content. We cannot say that all the observers have the same content, and we cannot say that they have not — not because we are ignorant, but because there would be no sense in either assertion.
> All the different individuals communicate to each other the structural forms, the patterns, and they can all agree about these, but . . . about the ineffable content they can neither agree nor disagree. (*GA* pp. 208–9, *PP* p. 334.)

It is interesting to compare Schlick's position with that of Locke. According to Locke, people commonly think that their words have intersubjective meanings: 'they suppose their words to be marks of the ideas in the minds also of other men with whom they communicate'; whereas the truth of the matter is that meanings are subjective: 'words in their primary and immediate signification stand for nothing but *the ideas in the mind of him that uses them*'.[20] But according to Schlick the common error, and the truth of the matter, are just the other way round. A person may think of his words as 'standing for the contents in his visual field', but this, says Schlick, is a mistake; his statement 'expresses the structure of the observed fact . . . but it does not convey the content "blue" or any other' (*GA* p. 208, *PP* p. 333).

Locke was not seriously worried about intersubjectivity of meaning, but Schlick was.[21] In his account of language in the lectures, Schlick tried to do three things: to explain the way in which meanings are intersubjective; to show how empirical statements can correspond with empirical facts; and to accommodate the subjectivity of experience. The first two aims were, he thought, satisfied by what he said about sameness of structure: on the one hand between the statements of different speakers, and on the other hand between statements and facts. But there is a tension between the first two aims and the third.

---

[20] Locke, *Essay*, 3.2.2, 3.2.4.

[21] Locke disposes of the matter in 2.32.15 of the *Essay*.

The second aim, put more explicitly, is to satisfy the empiricist principle that the meaning of a statement must be confined to a corresponding item of empirical reality. Formerly this was thought of as the speaker's experience; now it is taken to be the structure of a fact. Here, thought Schlick, he had found something which has the right sort of closeness of fit (as we may call it) with the meaning of a statement. But this means that the third ingredient, subjective experience, has no place in language at all. Content, as Schlick insisted, is incommunicable. According to Locke, what happens in communication is that men use words 'as it were, to bring out their *ideas* and lay them before the view of others' (*Essay* 3.2.2). Such an account of language would not have satisfied Schlick, and he did not think that content could be 'brought out' or 'laid before the view of others' in any sense. But now we may wonder how the talk about content can contribute anything at all to Schlick's account of language and reality. Moreover, how can *he* communicate with the reader about that which is beyond communication?

Schlick was aware of this tension. 'There is', he wrote, 'no proposition about content, there cannot be any. In other words: it would be best not to use the word "content" at all.' His 'only excuse for using the word' was, he said, that this 'forbidden road' would take the reader to a point where he could get 'a first view of the land before him' (*GA* p. 176, *PP* pp. 306–7, *ER* p. 149). This passage is reminiscent of Wittgenstein's claim in the *Tractatus*, that in the propositions of that work he had given the reader a sort of ladder, enabling him to 'see the world aright', but which 'he must, so to speak, throw away . . . after he has climbed up it' (*Tractatus* 6.54). But as we shall see in section 7.6, the reasons for this remark in the *Tractatus* were different from those of Schlick. Here it would be more appropriate to quote a remark from Wittgenstein's later writings: 'A nothing would serve just as well as a something about which nothing could be said' (*PI* 304).

Schlick's argument for the existence of an incommunicable content relies on certain conceptions of what it is to communicate or convey something. In one passage he asks the reader to suppose that he had sent a green leaf to a friend.

'He will see and touch *the same* leaf that I have seen and touched before, the leaf "itself" will have been transported to him'. By contrast, it makes no sense to suppose that 'I could take the greenness of a colour which I am experiencing out of my own consciousness and put it into somebody else's', so that he would have 'the green itself' (*GA* pp. 170–1, *PP* pp. 301–2, *ER* p. 143).

In another passage Schlick made a contrast between knowledge and enjoyment. Knowledge he regarded as structured in the same way as statements, and therefore communicable by means of them. If a person wants knowledge about the Egyptian pyramids, for example, it can be communicated to him in the form of statements. But enjoyment is a different matter.

> The enjoyment we have when looking at the pyramids cannot be communicated and there is no substitute for it. And it remains true that it is neither the highest degree of knowledge nor even its lowest degree, but simply the indescribable that precedes everything else. (*GA* p. 193, *PP* pp. 320–1.)

There is some truth in these contrasts. Enjoyment cannot be conveyed in the sense in which a leaf can be conveyed, for example by being sent in a box. Nor can it be communicated in the same sense as knowledge. To communicate knowledge to someone is to bring it about that he has the same knowledge as oneself; but this is not true of enjoyment. But it does not follow that enjoyment is an indescribable something which cannot be communicated. On the contrary, the enjoyment of looking at the pyramids, for example, has been described and communicated in innumerable travel-books and postcards to the family. If Schlick will not allow this as an example of describing and communicating, it is not because it fails to be one, but because it does not conform to his model.

Schlick's rejection of content from the domain of language is not very far away from Carnap's rejection of the 'material mode' of language, in which there had been reference to experience. But Schlick remained throughout an opponent of the coherence theory. Truth, he maintained, is a relation between propositions and something other than propositions: we 'compare our propositions with reality'. But the reality in question must be that of structure and not content. 'A proposition will be verified, the truth will be established, if the structure is the same as the structure of the fact it tries to express' (*GA* p. 228, *PP* p. 349). We must now examine this side of Schlick's account.

What did Schlick mean by 'structure'? He explained that sameness of structure between a proposition and a fact is like that between equivalent statements in different languages. Thus a fact 'may be expressed in a thousand different languages, and the thousand different propositions will all have the same structure, and the fact which they express will have the same structure, too . . .' (*GA* p. 158, *PP* p. 290, *ER* p. 131). It appears that by 'structure' Schlick did not mean what one might at first have thought. It might be said, for example, that the statements 'Roses are red' and 'Violets are blue' have the same logical structure, in contrast, say, to the statement 'Roses are bigger than violets'. But the first two statements do not express the same fact, notwithstanding their sameness of structure. It begins to look as if 'same structure' is merely another expression for 'same meaning', as in the case of equivalent statements in different languages, described by Schlick. But this cannot be right, because facts do not have meaning in the sense in which statements do. We can say that the statements 'It is raining' and 'Il pleut' have the same meaning, but we cannot say that the statement 'It is raining' has the same meaning as the fact that it is raining.

As we have seen, Schlick spoke of 'comparing' statements with facts. When Hempel objected that a statement can only be compared with other statements, he replied: 'We can compare anything to anything if we choose'.[22] The difficulty, however, is not about *whether* statements can be compared with facts, but about *how* this is to be done — about the meaning of 'compare' in this case. One may be asked to com-

---

[22] 'Facts and Propositions', *Analysis* (1935), *PP* p. 401, *ER* p. 197. Hempel's claim that a statement can only be compared with other statements is akin to Berkeley's remark: 'an idea can be like nothing but another idea' (*Principles of Human Knowledge*, IX).

pare chalk with cheese or cabbages with kings, but unless one were told in which respect to compare them, one would not know what to do. Two ways (among others) in which statements may be compared are in respect of their meanings and of their truth values (whether true or false). But a statement cannot be compared with a fact in these ways, for facts do not have truth-values and are not meaningful (or meaningless) in the way that statements are. In his *Analysis* paper, Schlick took as an example the statement 'This cathedral has two spires', which he found in his Baedeker travel-guide. He was, he said, 'able to compare it with "reality" by looking at the cathedral' (*PP* p. 400, *ER* p. 197). Hempel, in a further rejoinder, admitted that one way of comparing them would be by treating both the cathedral and the printed statement as physical objects and saying, for example, that the statement 'contains more parts, called "words", than the cathedral has spires'.[23] But such comparison has nothing to do with the *verification* of the statement.

Schlick's original idea, as we have seen, was that statements and facts are compared in respect of 'structure'; but, as I have pointed out, it is not clear what could be meant by structure in this context. It is essential to Schlick's empiricism that the meaning of statements must be wholly accounted for by a reality other than statements. Corresponding to a true statement there must be, he thinks, an item of reality, such that the two can be described as 'the same'. This leads him to postulate a relation — sameness of structure between statements and facts — which is to fulfil this requirement. But he does not explain how this relation is to be understood. Hempel also thought of verification as a matter of comparing. But since, as he had argued, the appropriate kind of comparing could take place only between statements and not between statements and facts, he concluded that the correct account of verification and truth was that of the coherence theory. But the choice between different objects of comparison need not be made. When Schlick verified the statement in his Baedeker he did indeed do it, not by looking at

[23] 'Some remarks on "Facts" and Propositions', *Analysis* (1935), *ER* p. 202.

other statements, but by looking at the cathedral. But that
does not mean that he *compared* the statement with the
cathedral, and found them to be in some respect *the same.*
If this goes against the tenets of empiricism, then it is the
latter that must give way.

6 The Unity of Science

6.1 ENCYCLOPEDIA, REDUCTIONISM AND THE 'THING-LANGUAGE'

In 1938 there appeared the opening sections of a work to be known as the *International Encyclopedia of Unified Science.* This project, originally conceived by Otto Neurath, was to comprise some twenty-six volumes, each containing ten monographs contributed by different scientists and philosophers. They would deal with various aspects of the philosophy of science, but with particular emphasis on the unity of the different sciences. The general idea of such an Encyclopedia was discussed at length at the First International Congress for the Unity of Science, held in Paris in 1935, and the Congress voted its approval.

Neurath intended the work as an international enterprise, with editions in English, French and German, and with contributions from Asiatic as well as Western writers. It appears, from letters written to Charles Morris,[1] that he thought of the work as similar in historical importance to the great French *Encyclopédie* begun under the direction of Diderot in the eighteenth century. Neurath died in 1945 and the editorship was taken over by Carnap and Morris. By 1969 two volumes of the work, containing 19 monographs between them, had been published, under the title *Foundations of the Unity of Science.*

It appears that Neurath was at work on the project as early as 1920 and perhaps earlier. The conception on which it is based is, in any case, apparent in such writings as the Vienna Circle's 'manifesto' of 1929, entitled 'The Scientific Concep-

---

[1] Most of the details given in this and the preceding paragraph are taken from an introduction by Morris to the 1969 edition of vol. I of the *Encyclopedia* (*Foundations of the Unity of Science,* ed. O. Neurath et al.).

tion of the World' and written by Neurath with the collaboration of Carnap and Hahn. Here we read that 'the aim' of the scientific conception is a 'unified science'; an aim which was to be attained by applying the 'method of logical analysis' to empirical data. The meaning of every scientific statement and every scientific concept, of whatever branch of science, must be analysable step by step to concepts of a common basic type, 'referring to the given itself'.[2]

One of those who attended the Paris congress but did not vote with the majority was Sir Karl Popper. Described by Neurath as 'the official opposition' of the Vienna Circle, he was against the whole idea of the *Encyclopedia.* Popper predicted that it would merely 'turn out to be another series of *Erkenntnis* articles', without achieving the integration desired by Neurath.[3]

The first of these predictions was perhaps unduly pessimistic. Certainly the *Encyclopedia,* even to the limited extent to which it has been realized, contains a far greater richness of ideas that one would find in the old numbers of *Erkenntnis.* This is not surprising, given that the latter were largely written by a closely knit group and within a relatively short period. But just as the *Encyclopedia* is more than a mere rehash of Vienna Circle ideas, so it presents a view that is less integrated than the latter and, if anything, further removed from the realization of Neurath's ideal. What we find are so many separate pieces by various authors, all, admittedly, interested more or less in topics of the kind discussed in the Circle, but presenting no unified picture of science or the world. A reader of Thomas Kuhn's *The Structure of Scientific Revolutions* (1962), for example, may be struck by it as an interesting and original view of the nature of science, while hardly noticing that it is part (vol. 2, No. 2) of the great work of unification that Neurath had launched.

---

[2] 'Wissenschaftliche Weltauffassung – der Wiener Kreis', *Erkenntnis* (1931); reprinted in H. Schleichert (ed.), *Logischer Empirismus – der Wiener Kreis*; see pp. 207, 211. This is the paper that was specially bound and presented to Schlick, as mentioned in chapter 1.

[3] See Popper's contribution in Schilpp (ed.), *The Philosophy of Rudolf Carnap*, pp. 200–1.

Neurath tried to explain his intentions in an introduction to the work. The *Encyclopedia,* he wrote, 'aims to show how various scientific activities such as observation, experimentation and reasoning can be synthetized, and how all these together help to evolve a unified science' (p. 2). The 'general purpose ... is to bring together material pertaining to the scientific enterprise as a whole' (p. 24). After a wide-ranging account of the development of science and philosophy through the centuries, he looks forward to the fruitful co-operation of scientists in the future. 'The maximum of co-operation — that is the program! This co-operation strives to elaborate the framework of unified science' (p. 24). But there is little in Neurath's introduction to tell us what exactly these phrases mean. Nor is it made clear whether he has a philosophical thesis about science (that science is 'one'), as distinct from his historical account and his hope that workers in different branches of science will co-operate with one another.

A philosophical foundation for the *Encyclopedia* is, however, provided by Carnap in an introductory essay entitled 'Logical Foundations of the Unity of Science'. Carnap tries to show that the different sciences are one, not in a sense depending on the actual or future co-operation of scientists, but because of 'the unity of the language of science' (p. 52, *ER* p. 120). His thesis is that (whether scientists realize it or not) there is a basic kind of language to which the statements of all the various sciences are reducible. The apparent variety of the concepts used masks, according to Carnap, an underlying unity; there is, at bottom, only one language of science and in that sense only one science.

In his belief that this is so, and in his evident satisfaction in this belief, Carnap is following a long and continuing tradition in philosophy — one that has been important in the thought of empiricists and rationalists alike. Thus Locke assures us that

all those sublime thoughts, which tower above the clouds and reach as high as heaven itself, take their rise and footing here: in all that great extent wherein the mind wanders, in those remote speculations it may seem to be elevated with, it stirs not one jot beyond those *ideas* which *sense* or *reflection* have offered for its contemplation (*Essay*, 2.1.24).

The rationalist Leibniz, speaking of 'remedies of the mind' which assist the 'power of thinking', declared:

> It is the greatest remedy for the mind if a few thoughts can be found from which infinite others arise in order, just as from the assumption of a few numbers, from one to ten, all the other numbers can be derived in order.[4]

Carnap's belief and hope was that all the various sciences could be reduced to a basic set of terms.

Now one might think that this is such a wide-ranging idea that Carnap would need a large part of the *Encyclopedia* to himself to demonstrate it. Gilbert Ryle once wrote: 'There is no such animal as "Science". There are scores of sciences.' And he went on to mention some of them: philology, botany, entomology, meteorology, geology, physiology, physics (*Dilemmas* pp. 71–3). It would not be difficult to extend the list, both in length and in variety. Is Carnap really going to apply his thesis to all the sciences that might be listed? No; for it soon becomes evident that he has in mind a simple way of classifying the sciences which, he thinks, will enable him to establish the main points of his thesis in an overall way.

In a section headed 'The Main Branches of Science', Carnap begins by distinguishing 'formal' from 'empirical' science. The former, consisting of logic and mathematics, is left aside for treatment in another place. He next distinguishes biological from non-biological science, appropriating the name 'physics' for the whole of the latter. Used in this broad sense, 'physics' is to comprehend 'both systematic and historical investigations within this field, thus including chemistry, mineralogy, astronomy, geology (which is historical), meteorology etc.'. However, a few lines later it appears that

[4] 'Of an Organum or Ars Magna of Thinking', *Leibniz Philosophical Writings*, ed. G. H. R. Parkinson, p. 1.

Carnap's first substantial point is about physics in the narrower (i.e. normal) sense, leaving the rest of 'physics' out of account. There is, he points out, a way in which physics (in the normal sense) is fundamental relative to other sciences, especially biology. 'The biologist has to know these laws of physics in studying the processes in organisms'; whereas the laws of biology do not have a corresponding place in the study of physics. 'Biology presupposes physics, but not vice versa' (*Encyclopedia* p. 46, *ER* p. 115).

Carnap's next proposal is to classify under 'biology' (using this 'in the wider sense') both 'what is usually called biology' and what is 'usually called psychology and social science'. As we shall see, Carnap devotes much attention to what he calls psychology. His claim is that 'psychological' statements — ordinary statements about what people feel and think — are 'reducible', together with scientific statements of all kinds, to a common kind of language which he calls the 'thing-language'. The thing-language is what we use 'in speaking about the properties of the observable (inorganic) things surrounding us'. It is to be distinguished from the language of physics where observation is less immediate. Thus

> terms like 'hot' and 'cold' may be regarded as belonging to the thing-language, but not 'temperature' because its determination requires the application of a technical instrument; further 'heavy' and 'light' (but not 'weight'); 'red', 'blue' etc.; 'large', 'small', 'thick', 'thin', etc. (*Encyclopedia*, pp. 52–3, *ER* p. 121).

These 'observable thing-predicates' are to be taken as basic, says Carnap; even such substance-terms as 'stone', 'water' and 'sugar', though belonging to the thing-language, are reducible to observable thing-predicates.

Carnap is careful to distinguish his thesis of 'reducibility' from the earlier view, held by him and other verificationists, which we noted in ection 4.1. According to that view, a meaningful statement is analysable into a set of observation-statements; these statements — or the corresponding observations — constituting the meaning of the statement. Such a view, as we saw, had been expressed in Waismann's 'Theses'.

It was also applied, in that work, to 'psychological' statements, for example about a person's anger.

> A proposition cannot say more than what is established by the method of verification. If I say 'My friend is angry' and establish that this is so through his behaving in a certain observable way, then what I *mean* by the proposition is merely that he is showing this behaviour. And if I mean more, then I cannot say what this 'more' consists in. A proposition only says what it says, and nothing beyond that.
> *The sense of a proposition is the method of its verification.*[5]

This is not the sort of view that Carnap is now defending. His view now is expressed primarily as a thesis about words. A meaningful word (or term), he maintains, must be reducible to 'observable thing-predicates' by means of 'reduction statements'. Given the term 'electric charge', for example, we first introduce a typical statement in which that term is applied, such as 'The body x has an electric charge at the time t'. Then the following would be a suitable reduction-statement: 'If a light body y is placed near x at time t, then: x has an electric charge at $t \equiv y$ is attracted by x at t' (p. 50, *ER* p. 119).[6] Such a reduction-statement, says Carnap, is 'so to speak, a conditional definition' of the term in question.

The terms in the reduction-statement just quoted are capable of further reduction; and Carnap speaks in this connection of 'reduction chains'. Sometimes, he says, a scientific term will be reducible to other scientific terms, and these in turn until we arrive at terms of the thing-language. These again may need further reduction before we reach the final goal of observable thing-predicates. As examples of terms within the thing-language needing such reduction, Carnap

---

[5] *WWK* p. 244, *ER* p. 27. This passage (except for the final sentence) was omitted from the quotation on page 24. The 'earlier' view had also been taken by Carnap in his 'Psychology in Physical Language', *Erkenntnis* (1932–33).

[6] The symbol '$\equiv$' means that each of the statements preceding and following it implies the other.

gives substance-terms such as 'stone', 'water' etc., and dispositional terms such as 'elastic', 'soluble' and the like. In both cases, he says, it must be possible to achieve reduction to observable thing-predicates by means of reduction statements of the kind I have quoted.

Turning to what he calls psychology, Carnap maintains that such terms as 'anger' are reducible to the thing-language in the same sort of way as the terms of theoretical physics, for example 'electric charge'. In this case, however, the relevant reduction-statements will be about a person's behaviour. 'The logical nature of the psychological terms becomes clear by an analogy with those physical terms which are introduced by reduction statements of the conditional form' (*Encyclopedia*, p. 59, *ER* p. 126). (Carnap's treatment of psychological terms will be discussed in the next section.)

In its use of conditionals Carnap's reductionism is akin to the operationism and phenomenalism discussed in sections 4.7 and 4.2. In this respect they all differ from the 'original' view, as given in the quotation from Waismann, where meaning is represented in categorical terms. A further difference in Carnap's thesis, however, is that it is primarily about words as opposed to statements. He is not now saying that a categorical statement can be translated into a set, possibly infinite, of hypothetical statements; his claim is, rather, that the meaning of a word is given by the relevant reduction-statements, and that this accounts for its meaning in all other statements.

Having examined the main branches of science as he sees them, Carnap asserts: 'there is a *unity of language* in science, viz. a common reduction basis for the terms of all branches of science, this basis consisting of a very narrow and homogeneous class of terms of the physical thing-language' (*Encyclopedia*, p. 61, *ER* p. 128).

In spite of the differences just noted, we have here a fundamental continuity with the earlier views. There is still the conviction that all language is reducible, by some uniform method, to a set of basic terms; these terms forming, in Carnap's words, 'a very narrow and homogeneous class'. This they do because they are, in some essential way, all alike. And since (as was thought) all the rest of language is reducible to these basic terms by some uniform method, it follows that all specimens of language are, in the last resort, essentially alike. This is true equally of Carnap's reductionism and of the earlier analysis of statements into verification-statements or acts of verification. It is also true of the account of language that Wittgenstein had given in the *Tractatus*. On this point we find a crucial change between the *Tractatus* and the *Philosophical Investigations*. In the latter work Wittgenstein imagines someone objecting that he has failed to say, as he had in the *Tractatus*, what 'the essence' of language is, 'what is common to all these activities, and what makes them into language or part of language'. He replies:

> And this is true. — Instead of producing something common to all that we call language, I am saying that these phenomena have no one thing in common, which makes us use the same word for all, — but that they are *related* to one another in many different ways (*PI* 65).

In another passage he writes that 'what we call "sentence" and "language" has not the formal unity that I imagined, but is [a] family of structures more or less related to one another' (*PI* 108).

One of the difficulties of the earlier conception of language is shown by Carnap's attempt to identify his 'very narrow and homogeneous class' of basic terms. As we saw, he gives as examples the terms 'hot' and 'cold', 'heavy' and 'light', 'red' and 'blue', 'large' and 'small'. But in what sense do they form a homogeneous class? There are all sorts of logical and epistemological differences between them. It might be said, for example, that 'hot' and 'heavy' are both objects of feeling. But feeling that the bathwater is hot is not like feeling that a suitcase is heavy. To feel the former requires a sense of touch; but this is neither necessary nor sufficient for the latter.[7] On the other hand, it is also possible to *see* that a thing is heavy, say by observing its motion; but this is a different kind of observation from seeing that it is red or blue. Colours, again, have a different logic from that of the other examples. In the case of the latter (large and small, hot and

_____
[7] A similar point was made about impenetrability in section 4.3. See pages 58–9.

cold etc.) we have gradations of more and less; but this is not the way in which primary colours are related to one another. Finally and more generally, the application of the predicates will depend on circumstances in a variety of ways. Whether an animal is large or small will depend on whether it is being compared with others of its kind or with animals of another kind (and if so, which). The description of a thing as warm will depend on whether one is talking about one's dinner or the water in the swimming pool. The colour-word 'white' will denote different colours in 'white paint', 'white wine' and 'white skin'.

The objection to Carnap's examples is not only that they are not homogeneous, but also that they are not basic; for as we have seen, a variety of knowledge of circumstances and knowledge of other concepts is presupposed in the correct application of his predicates. This is not to say that there is no sense whatever in the idea of a thing-language. Carnap is right in seeing important distinctions between the language of scientific theory and the language of ordinary things, and between language requiring a use of instruments (such as 'temperature') and language not requiring this (such as 'hot' and 'cold'). He has not, however, succeeded in showing that there is a homogeneous class of basic terms, such as would give substance to the idea of a 'unified science'.

The difficulty exists, as we have seen, even among the examples given by Carnap; but all sorts of other terms would seem to qualify for inclusion in the thing-language if the only criteria are the ones just mentioned. In his *Encyclopedia* essay Carnap introduced the thing-language, informally, as the one we use in speaking of ordinary physical things; giving examples of what he had in mind. But a more formal account had been attempted in 'Testability and Meaning':

A predicate 'P' of a language L is called *observable* for an organism (e.g. a person) N, if, for suitable arguments, e.g. 'b', N is able under suitable circumstances to come to a decision with the help of a few observations about a full sentence, say 'P(b)', i.e. to a confirmation of either 'P(b)' or '~P(b)' of such a high degree that he will either accept or reject 'P(b)'. (P. 63.)

Carnap admitted that this explanation was 'necessarily vague', because one may be 'more or less able to decide a certain sentence quickly'. But he seems not to have realized what a great variety of predicates would be admitted by such a formula. Why should not, for example, the terms 'aircraft-carrier' and 'impressionist painting' qualify for inclusion?[8] Yet one would hardly consider these as belonging, in any sense, to the basic part of language. Again, why should we accept that a term such as 'angry' does not belong to the basic part of language, but is in need of reduction? Admittedly Carnap stipulated that the thing-language is that used for inorganic things, and this would exclude 'angry'. But there seems to be no good reason for excluding it, according to the criterion just quoted. Nor do we have here a scientific-theoretical term, or one whose application requires a use of instruments. (This point may also be made about the previous examples.) Nevertheless it seems clear that 'angry' is a very different sort of word from either 'red' or 'heavy'.

Why should it be thought that the whole of language must have a homogeneous basis — a class of terms which are all alike and to which all others are reducible? Carnap used a 'practical' argument for his thesis. The unity of language was, he said, 'of the greatest practical importance' in the ordinary affairs of life; and he illustrated this by reference to the different kinds of knowledge that go into predicting the sales of a motor-car. Here, he pointed out,

> we have to combine knowledge about the function of the motor, the effect of gases and vibration on the human organism, the ability of persons to learn a certain technique, their willingness to spend so much money for so much service, the development of the economic situation, etc. (*Encyclopedia*, pp. 61–2, *ER* p. 128.)

He went on: 'If now the terms of the different branches had no logical connection between one another, such as is sup-

---

[8] A similar point may be made even about the theoretical terms of science. See Peter Achinstein, 'The Problem of Theoretical Terms', *American Philosophical Quarterly* (1965).

plied by the homogeneous reduction basis', then such predictions would be impossible. Carnap is right in maintaining that there are logical connections between the language used in various branches of knowledge; in that sense the unity of language is a fact which hardly requires argument. But this leaves open the question about the nature of the connections. It does not follow that they must all be of one kind or that there must be a homogeneous class of terms to which all others are reducible. According to the later Wittgenstein, as we have seen, the different phenomena of language are 'related to one another'; but they are so 'in many different ways'.

6.2 PSYCHOLOGY AND THE UNITY OF SCIENCE

The reduction of 'psychological' terms to the thing-language was, as we have noted, one of Carnap's main concerns. There were, he thought, at least two ways in which this could be achieved: the way of behaviour and the way of biology or physiology. 'If for anger we knew a sufficient and necessary criterion to be found by a physiological analysis of the nervous system or other organs, then we could define "angry" in terms of the biological language' (*Encyclopedia* p. 56, *ER* p. 124). These biological terms would be further reducible until finally one arrived at a basis of observable thing-predicates. But on the whole Carnap's preference was for the other alternative, behaviour, where the correlations with anger did not await scientific discovery but were a matter of common knowledge. He believed that all psychological terms could be rendered into reduction-statements about behaviour and that, furthermore, the latter could be expressed in terms of the inorganic thing-language.

There are a number of reasons for and against the two approaches. The behaviourist approach seems, on the face of it, the more natural application of verificationism to psychological statements. We do verify that a person is angry by observing his behaviour; and as we saw on page 108, Waismann regarded the behaviourist interpretation of 'My friend is angry' as a typical application of the verification principle. There is also, as was pointed out on page 109, a close parallel between behaviourism and phenomenalism, with its use of conditional statements. A similar parallel was claimed by Carnap in connection with his method of reduction-statements.

> If Robinson Crusoe is angry and then dies before anybody comes to his island, nobody except himself ever knows of this single occurrence of anger. But anger of the same kind, occurring with other persons, may be studied and ascertained by a behaviouristic method, if circumstances are favourable. (Analogy: if an electrically charged raindrop falls into the ocean without an observer or suitable recording instrument in the neighbourhood, nobody will ever know of that charge. But a charge of the same kind can be found under suitable circumstances by certain observations.) (*Encyclopedia,* p. 58, *ER* p. 125.)

But not every feeling manifests itself in a typical kind of behaviour as anger (in some cases at least) does. There is no obvious kind of behaviour that goes with feelings of nostalgia, pride or gratitude, for example. Perhaps it will be thought that in these cases the relevant behaviour consists simply in *saying* that one has the feeling in question.[9] But this will not do as an analysis of meaning, since the term to be analysed will occur in the sentences in which one says this.

In the case of the 'biological' view, on the other hand, the question of physical manifestations is one for the scientist — 'to be found by a physiological analysis of the nervous system or other organs'. The attraction of this view is not that the analysis has been accomplished; it is the widespread assumption that it could be accomplished, given enough research — that, in other words, there *are* physiological conditions specific to anger and to every other psychological term. An obvious disadvantage of this view is that the assumption may be wrong. There are indeed philosophical and not merely empirical grounds for questioning it. But leaving these

---

[9] Compare Carnap in Schilpp (ed.), *The Philosophy of Rudolf Carnap,* p. 886: '... there is a possible behaviouristic symptom for the toothache — if no other, then at least the utterance of the sentence mentioned.'

aside, there is the further difficulty that on this view knowing the meaning of an ordinary word like 'anger' would be dependent on having the relevant scientific knowledge.[10]

Carnap's interest in the reduction of psychological terms was not peculiar to the *Encyclopedia* essay, but showed itself in many other writings and in the course of different versions of his verificationism and reductionism. He believed throughout that the different uses of language could all be shown to conform to a single model, and that this must be true particularly of psychological language, no less than any other.

We have already noted some of the difficulties of Carnap's general thesis. But there is a special problem about psychological terms. It was a problem that worried Wittgenstein when he went to lecture at Cambridge in the early 1930s. Wittgenstein's class became known as the 'toothache club', from his frequent use of toothache as an example. But the questions he raised about toothache also apply to psychological terms, such as those discussed by Carnap. 'When we say "He has toothache" ', asked Wittgenstein, 'is it correct to say that his toothache is only his behaviour, whereas when I talk about my toothache I am not talking about my behaviour?'. 'Is another person's toothache "toothache" in the same sense as mine?'

In trying to find an answer to this question or these questions, he said first that it was clear and admitted that what verifies or is a criterion for 'I have toothache' is quite different from what verifies or is a criterion for 'He has toothache', and soon added that, since this is so, the meanings of 'I have toothache' and 'He has toothache' must be different.[11]

---

[10]This difficulty has been avoided by a more recent version of physicalism, the 'contingent identity thesis'. According to this, ignorance of the scientific facts does not affect one's ability to know the meaning of such terms as 'anger'. Just as we may know the meaning of 'evening star' without knowing that the evening star is identical with the morning star, so (it is claimed) we may know the meaning of 'anger' without being aware that anger is a brain-process.

[11]G. E. Moore, 'Wittgenstein's Lectures in 1930–33', *Mind* (1955), p. 11; reprinted in Moore's *Philosophical Papers*.

This conclusion (that the meanings must be different) might be acceptable if we were speaking of a *partial* difference of verification, and a partial difference of meanings corresponding to it. Such would be the difference between, for example, the sentences 'I have a coin in my pocket' and 'He has a coin in his pocket'. But the difference of verification between the two sentences about toothache is more fundamental. Wittgenstein went on to say that the very meaning of 'verify' could not be the same in both cases; and, on a later occasion, that 'there is no such thing as a verification for "I have", since the question "How do you know that you have toothache?" is nonsensical'.[12]

It was this difficulty about the verification of certain first-person statements which, as Moore reports, drew Wittgenstein away from verificationism. A different course was taken by Carnap, who argued that the difference between the first- and third-person statements was not really fundamental. In 'Testability and Meaning' he admitted that a person N_1 'can confirm more directly than N_2 a sentence concerning N_1's feelings, thoughts etc.'. But, he went on, 'we now believe, on the basis of physicalism, that the difference, although very great and very important for practical life, is only a matter of degree' (*TM* p. 79). In a later writing he maintained that 'a person's awareness of his own state of imagining, feeling etc. must be recognized as a kind of observation, in principle not different from external observation, and therefore as a legitimate source of knowledge'.[13]

What did Carnap mean by 'observation' in these contexts? Sometimes he thought of it as introspection, sometimes as observation of bodily conditions. If the latter view is taken, then we can readily understand the claim that the difference between N_1 and N_2 is 'only a matter of degree'. Such a view had been expounded by Carnap in his important earlier paper 'Psychology in Physical Language'.[14] Taking as his example the assertion 'I am now excited', he maintained that it would

---

[12] A similar point was made by Lazerowitz against Ayer, as we saw on page 40.

[13] *Minnesota Studies in the Philosophy of Science,* ed. H. Feigl, vol. 1, pp. 70–1.

[14] *Erkenntnis* (1932–33); a translation appears in *LP.*

be made on the basis of protocol statements such as 'I feel my hands trembling', 'I see my hands trembling' and 'I hear my voice quavering'. These observations, he claimed, were available to others in the same sort of way as to oneself, being observations of a physical object, my body. Hence the statement 'I am now excited' has 'the same content as the physical statement "My body is now in that condition which, both under my own observation and that of others, exhibits such and such characteristics of excitement"' (*LP* p. 191). Here it appears that the difference between myself and others is merely a difference between different individuals, all using the same type of method of verification. It may be that some of them — myself particularly — are better placed than others to make the necessary observations; but the difference is 'only a matter of degree' and not one of 'principle'.

In the opening pages of this paper Carnap warned the reader that he must be prepared to set aside a certain 'emotional resistance' to the physicalist view. He was, he said, in the same sort of position as thinkers like Copernicus, Darwin, Marx and Freud. Their views had been thought to diminish the dignity of man and were therefore denied 'a sober, objective examination' when they first appeared. But no emotion is needed in order to see that Carnap's account is at odds with the normal use of such statements as 'I am excited' and 'I have a toothache'. One does not arrive at these statements by observing one's own body, nor by any other observation. That is why, as Wittgenstein pointed out, 'the question "How do you know you have toothache?" is nonsensical'.

But if the bodily account is rejected, what is the correct view? The main alternative, as Carnap saw it, was that of introspection. According to this view, when a person says, for example, that he is angry, he relies on a special kind of 'self-observation, or "introspection"', whereby 'he grasps, in a direct manner, something non-physical' (*LP* p. 192). The kind of self-observation that proponents of this view have in mind differs from observation of physical objects, in that its objects can be observed only by the person concerned. You and I can see my hands trembling, but only I can observe the 'something non-physical' which is my feeling of anger, excitement or pain.

This view of the matter leads, however, to the notorious problem of 'other minds'. If my feeling is something known only to me, then how can I attribute a similar feeling to you? How can I tell that when you say you are angry, you feel what I mean by that word? This problem also has a traditional solution, a solution that was given and then rejected in Carnap's paper. He presented the traditional view as follows:

When I myself am angry, I not only act out the behaviour-pattern of an angry man, I experience a special *feeling* of anger. If, consequently, I observe someone else acting out the same behaviour-pattern I may, on grounds of analogy, conclude (if not with certainty, at least with probability) that he too, besides acting as he does, now has a *feeling* of anger (which is not meant as a physical state of affairs). (*LP* p. 176.)[15]

Carnap criticized this argument by comparing it with another.

. . . let us consider an everyday argument from analogy. I see a box of matches of a certain shape, size and colour. I discover that it contains matches. I find another box of similar appearance, and now, by analogy, draw the probability inference that it too contains matches. Our critic believes that the argument from analogy he presents is of the same logical form . . . But this is not the case. In our critic's argument, the conclusion is *meaningless* – a mere pseudo-sentence. For, being a sentence about other minds, not to be physically interpreted, it is in principle not testable . . . That the second box also contains matches may in principle be tested . . . The two analogous sentences 'The first box contains matches' and 'The second box contains matches' are both logically and epistemologically of the same sort. This is why the analogy holds here. The case is different with 'I am angry' and 'That person is angry'. (*LP* p. 176.)[16]

[15] For a classic statement of this view, see J. S. Mill, *An Examination of Sir William Hamilton's Philosophy,* ch. XII.

[16] It is interesting to compare this passage with Wittgenstein's beetle-in-the-box example, PI 293.

Carnap's argument is typical of the verificationist approach. If all that I can observe of the other person's anger is his behaviour, then the meaning of 'He is angry' must be confined to that behaviour. Any talk of something beyond that (about the 'special *feeling* of anger') will be '*meaningless* – a mere pseudo-sentence'. One does not, however, have to be a verificationist in order to be dissatisfied with the introspectionist view. If what I mean by 'anger' is an object of my introspection, then indeed it is hard to see how I could, meaningfully, ascribe that feeling to another person.

In later writings, as we saw, Carnap was more sympathetic to the introspectionist view. But this view and behaviourism are equally paradoxical and at odds with ordinary usage. The first, based on a non-physical 'self-observation', entails that it is meaningless to ascribe feelings to others. The second, based on observation of physical things, entails that in ascribing a feeling, whether to oneself or to others, one is talking about conditions of the body and nothing else. But both accounts are wrong in assuming that the ascription of feelings is always based on observation. When I say that I am angry or have a toothache, I do not do it on the basis of observation. Nevertheless, when you make these statements about yourself, I can verify them by observation. Both of these points are essential to a correct view of the concepts in question.

In his later philosophy Wittgenstein argued, not merely that the 'private' meaning of the introspectionist is (as Carnap had argued) inapplicable to other persons; but that it is no meaning at all.[17] There must be, he maintained, criteria whereby different people can ascribe words like 'anger' and 'pain' to one another; and these criteria are to be found in their behaviour. This does not mean, however, that such statements are translatable or reducible to statements about behaviour. As he had pointed out in the 1930–33 lectures, 'when we pity a man for having toothache, we are not pitying him for putting his hand to his cheek'.[18] The first- and third-person uses of these concepts are connected, but not in

---

[17] *Philosophical Investigations*, 243ff. For a detailed commentary, see my *Language and the Privacy of Experience*.

[18] *Mind* (1955), p. 12. Moore says that this was 'implied' by Wittgenstein.

a way that allows them to be accommodated in either the behaviourist's or the introspectionist's mould. The attempt to do so results in paradox, because both take an unduly uniform view of language. 'The paradox disappears only if we make a radical break with the idea that language always functions in one way, always serves the same purpose . . .' (*PI* 304). This break was made by Wittgenstein in his later philosophy.

There is another way in which our understanding of the language of feelings will be distorted if we try to force it into one mould or the other. Here we must notice a difference between the example of anger and that of toothache. If we ask someone why he is groaning, holding his cheek etc., he will probably answer that he has a toothache. Similarly, if we ask someone why he banged the door, he may reply that he felt angry. But in the second case another sort of answer might be given: he may answer by telling us *why he felt angry* – i.e. what he is angry about. Perhaps he will refer to something offensive that had been said or done to him. In giving such an answer he would be explaining both his feeling and his behaviour. The ability to give such an answer is essential in a way in which the behaviour is not. If he has no answer to the question 'What are you angry about?', then we could not say that he feels angry, even if his behaviour resembles that of an angry man. On the other hand, if he can answer it, then (assuming he is speaking sincerely) we can say that he is angry, even if no angry behaviour is in evidence. Similarly, even if we accept that there is an object of introspection called 'anger', we could not say that a person introspecting this object is angry, unless he can answer the question 'What about?'. Failing this, the statement 'I am angry' would leave us puzzled. But the case is different with pain. We do not have to have an answer to the question 'Why are you in pain?' in order to accept that someone is in pain, and to understand why he behaves as he does.

It is not clear how these points about the logic of anger could be accommodated within a uniform conception of language, such as that of Carnap's observable thing-predicates or the earlier observation-statements. An earlier empiricist— reductionist, Hume, had made a point of denying the logical connection between a feeling and its object. 'When I am angry', he wrote,

> I am actually possest with the passion, and in that emotion have no more a reference to any other object, than when I am thirsty, or sick, or more than five foot high. 'Tis impossible, therefore, that this passion can be oppos'd by, or be contradictory to truth and reason.[19]

Hume's reduction differed from that of the Logical Positivists in that the final terms of it were mental entities called 'simple impressions'; but the resulting failure to do justice to the diversity of language is the same. For, contrary to what Hume says, the question whether someone is angry is not like the question whether he is thirsty, or sick, or more than five feet high. (Nor, indeed, are the latter terms all of the same type — any more than Carnap's thing-predicates.) In the case of anger, and many other emotions, the 'reference to another object' does mean, contrary to Hume's denial, that 'this passion can be opposed by, or contradictory to, truth and reason'. We do sometimes reason with an angry person, pointing out that his reason for feeling angry is false or inadequate (as the case may be). And this connection with reasons is essential to understanding the concept of anger.[20]

  The point about reference to another object also means that it is misleading to speak of anger as a 'psychological term' (or as Hume does, a 'passion'). In saying that I am angry with my friend for what he did, I am not merely making a psychological statement about myself; I am also passing judgment of my friend's behaviour. Here we have a normative aspect of the language of emotions, involving

---

[19] *Treatise* 2.3.3., p. 415. It is interesting that Hume chose the same example, anger. But the issue of course also affects other emotions, such as fear, pride and sadness. It is also worth noting that Hume regarded it, apparently, as obvious that thirst has no 'reference to any other object' — as if one could feel thirst independently of wanting something to drink.

[20] It is true that Hume went on to admit that a passion may be *'accompany'd* with some judgment or opinion' and that the latter may be reasonable or unreasonable; but this, he held, did not affect his claim that the passion was itself a separate entity (an 'original existence', as he called it) and beyond the reach of reason.

criticism and justification; and this cannot be fitted into a physical description of the world, whether that of the physicist or that of Carnap's thing-language.[21]

These criticisms of the Hume—Carnap view of emotions are not necessarily criticisms of verificationism; they are criticisms of the uniform view of language which was commonly thought to follow from that doctrine. The points I have made about the connection with reasons do not mean that a feeling like anger is unverifiable; nor that the word has a 'private' meaning, as it appeared on the introspectionist view. On the contrary, if we take the verification principle without the uniform view of language, we can see it as making an important point about the meaning of 'anger'. The method of verification of 'He is angry', for example, will include questions about his reasons, such as I have indicated. This means that the method in this case will be of a different type from those used for 'thirsty', 'sick' or 'red'; and this difference will be a reflection of a difference of kinds of meaning, in accordance with the verification principle. We are still left, however, with the difficulty about applying the principle to statements about oneself, where there is no verification.

[21] '"Ought" expresses a kind of necessity and of connection with grounds which is found nowhere else in the whole of nature ... When we have the course of nature alone in view, *"ought"* has no meaning whatsoever. It is just as absurd to ask what ought to happen in the natural world as to ask what properties a circle ought to have. All that we are justified in asking is: what happens in nature? what are the properties of the circle?' (Kant, *Critique of Pure Reason*, A547).

7 *The Elimination of Metaphysics*

7.1 METAPHYSICS AND EXPERIENCE

One of the main concerns of Logical Positivism, as we have seen, was to provide a way of demarcating the meaningful statements of science and ordinary life from the 'pseudo-statements' of metaphysics. The previous chapters have been concerned mainly with the positive aspect – the problems about including statements of the former kind. We must now consider the negative side – the 'elimination of metaphysics'.

The word 'metaphysics' is perhaps even more difficult to define than the word 'science'. However, it may be useful to distinguish some of the kinds of statements which have been regarded, by verificationists and others, as metaphysical. There is, on the one hand, a distinction between what we may call professional and non-professional metaphysics. Sometimes the verificationists took for their target such examples as Heidegger's 'The nothing nothings' and Bradley's talk about 'the Absolute'.[1] Here we have professional philosophers making statements and pursuing arguments which lie beyond the purview of the ordinary person. But metaphysical beliefs and speculations are also common – perhaps inevitable – among non-philosophers. Some obvious examples are religious belief, thoughts about 'the meaning of life' and speculations about life after death. Such beliefs and speculations were also to be subjected to the new criterion.

On the other hand, we may distinguish between what may be called conscious and unconscious metaphysics. Philosophers like Bradley and Heidegger were conscious that they were dealing with a special subject-matter, one that is not amenable to ordinary or scientific criteria; and the same is

[1] M. Heidegger, *What is Metaphysics?*; F. H. Bradley, *Appearance and Reality*.

true of the examples, just given, of 'ordinary man's' metaphysics. But the ordinary man may also have beliefs or
assumptions which are metaphysical without his being aware
that they are. He may be surprised to hear, for example, that
his conception of the human mind commits him to a metaphysical doctrine called 'dualism', or that his beliefs about
physical objects make him (according to some philosophers
anyway) a 'realist'. These beliefs and assumptions too were to
be subjected to the verificationist critique.[2]

Perhaps the question of what should be included under
'metaphysics' is sufficiently answered by describing and considering some typical examples, as has been done above and
will be further done in this chapter. Another sort of problem
arises, however, about the word 'experience'. Consider such
statements as 'This house is haunted' and 'There is an in-
visible presence in this house'. It may seem as if these statements should be included with metaphysical discourse, being
about a 'spiritual' reality and not (it may be said) within the
purview of science. Yet if we ask someone why he says these
things, he may answer in a way that seems to suit the require-
ments of empiricism very well: he may refer to an *experience*
he has when in the house. But would this be an experience in
the sense intended by empiricists? Would it be a sense-
experience? It could be; such a person may speak of hearing
noises, for example. But he may also speak of experiences in
another sense, saying that he experiences, or is aware of, a
presence in the house, but not in a way that involves the
senses. (Perhaps he will say that he 'senses' or 'feels' something, but not meaning this in a tactual or other sense-organ
sense.)

Perhaps, however, an empiricist would be willing to admit
such statements as meaningful, forming part of the corpus of
empirical knowledge — especially if he considers that they
might become more regular than they are, with widespread
agreement among 'observers'.[3]

[2] Schlick's treatment of 'realism' was discussed in section 4.4.

[3] See M. Scriven, 'Explanations of the Supernatural' in *Philosophy and Psychical Research*, ed. S. C. Thakur.

Similar questions arise about religious experiences. Some people would say, for example, that they have experiences of God when praying or meditating. Or they may claim to experience things in the physical world in a special way.

The concept of God was discussed by Carnap in his paper 'The Elimination of Metaphysics through the Logical Analysis of Language'. Here he distinguished three phases of the concept. In the first, God was conceived as a corporeal being with a dwelling, say, on Mount Olympus. Statements about such a God, he said, are clearly meaningful on the verificationist view. Secondly, the word may designate 'a spiritual being, not having a human body, but somehow showing itself in the objects and processes of the visible world, and therefore empirically ascertainable'. Finally he distinguished a 'metaphysical' use of the word, having no empirical meaning of any sort, and therefore exposed to the verificationist's attack.[4]

It is, however, the second and not the third description that would be regarded by many believers as closest to their conception of God. They may regard the talk of God 'somehow showing himself' in the world as describing their experiences of God in the world — especially, perhaps, in the sphere of human relations. Or again, they may think of the matter in terms of ordinary empirical facts which are (in accordance with the criterion discussed in chapter 3) deducible from statements about God. That there are fish in the sea is a straightforward empirical fact, verifiable by believers and non-believers alike. It is, however, deducible from what we read about God in the first book of *Genesis*; for there we are told, both that God created the fish of the sea, and that he told them (with other creatures) to be fruitful and multiply. Even those who read the Bible in a less literal sense may cite certain empirical facts as evidence of a divine creator (using the 'argument from design'). It does not matter if the argu-

---

[4]*Erkenntnis*, vol. II, pp. 225–6. A translation appears in *LP*. Carnap's account here is reminiscent of that of the nineteenth century positivist Auguste Comte, who distinguished three stages in the development of human thought – a theological, a metaphysical and a 'scientific or positive' stage. See, e.g., the opening of his *Introduction to Positive Philosophy*.

ment itself is rejected, as it commonly is nowadays. All that
is needed to satisfy the deducibility criterion is that *if* there
is a divine creator, then certain things will be observable in
the world. This is enough to render the statement meaningful, whether or not it is true. Similar points can be made
about metaphysical doctrines other than those of religion.[5]

To bring his critique to bear on such doctrines, the verificationist will have to resort to analysis and not merely deduction. (This was the conclusion reached at the end of chapter
3.) He will have to say *what* such a statement means, as
opposed to merely determining whether it is meaningful or
not. This approach was indeed taken by Ayer when he considered statements about God.

> If the sentence 'God exists' entails no more than that cer-
> tain types of phenomena occur in certain sequences, then
> to assert the existence of a god will be simply equivalent
> to asserting that there is the requisite regularity in nature
> . . .
> If . . . a man tells me that the occurrence of thunder is
> alone both necessary and sufficient to establish the truth
> of the proposition that Jehovah is angry, I may conclude
> that, in his usage of words, the sentence 'Jehovah is angry'
> is equivalent to 'It is thundering'. (*LTL* pp. 152, 154.)

Here we see religious statements being 'cut down to size'
in accordance with empiricist principles: they mean no more
and no less than what is verifiable in the approved way. But
again, a religious person may speak of experiences of a very
different kind from those described in the above passage. In

---

[5] 'Thales, for example, would support the view that "the principle of the world is
water" by pointing out that when ice is heated, it turns into water, and even
Bradley . . . maintains that "the doctrine which I hold I hold largely because it
seems to me to remain more than others in harmony with life." ' John Passmore,
'Logical Positivism (II)' *Australasian Journal of Philosophy* (1944), p. 142. Compare Carnap in *Philosophy and Logical Syntax*, ch. 1: 'From the proposition:
"The Principle of the world is Water" we are not able to deduce any proposition
asserting any perceptions or feelings or experiences whatever which may be expected for the future. Therefore the proposition, "The Principle of the world is
Water", asserts nothing at all.' See also A. C. Ewing, 'Meaninglessness', *Mind*
(1937) p. 351.

a further passage Ayer spoke of 'mystical intuition'. He would not, he said, 'deny *a priori* that the mystic is able to discover truths by his own special methods'. But, he went on, the mystic's statements, like any others, 'must be subject to the test of actual experience' (*LTL* pp. 156–7). But is not the mystic's experience a specimen of 'actual experience'? We may also mention a kind of statement, sometimes made by religious people (whether or not we describe it as 'mystical'), such as 'God is in this place' and 'God reveals himself to us when we pray'. These are very different from statements like 'It is thundering' and 'This is white'; but it does not follow that they are not statements of experience. (We have already seen in previous chapters that the attempt to identify one basic type of phenomenon, word or statement proved futile. See especially chapter 6 and section 4.4.)

For most verificationists, especially those addicted to the 'unity of science', it would, no doubt, go against the grain to admit statements of religious experience as meaningful. But perhaps they should admit them just the same. This would still leave them free to wield their criterion against beliefs which are, or purport to be, beyond experience of any kind. Here again, however, they will be faced with problems of analysis. It will be hard to determine, for any given belief, just what are the connections (if any) with experiential statements of one kind or another. Nor would it do to put the onus of analysis wholly on the person holding the belief; for, as we saw in chapter 4, the analysis of even the most ordinary statements is a difficult and controversial matter, and beyond the ability of ordinary speakers of the language.

7.2 METAPHYSICS AND SCIENCE

We have seen that experience may play a role in connection with metaphysical beliefs as well as those of science. There are other, more general resemblances between metaphysics and science. About metaphysical beliefs it may be said that even if there is some connection with experience, the belief goes beyond experience. But, as we saw in section 4.7, the same may be said about theories of science. Such a theory

cannot be equated with the data by which it would be verified. One way in which a theory goes beyond the data is in
providing an exaplanation of them, as opposed to a mere
description or summary. The explanatory power of a theory
is one of the main reasons for adopting it. But metaphysical
theories may also be thought to have explanatory power. As
an example we may take empiricism itself. Consider this
famous passage from the start of John Locke's *Essay*:

> It is an established opinion amongst some men that there
> are in the *understanding* certain *innate principles,* some
> primary notions . . . characters, as it were, stamped upon
> the mind of man, which the soul receives in its very first
> being and brings into the world with it. It would be suf-
> ficient to convince unprejudiced readers of the falseness of
> this supposition, if I should only show (as I hope I shall in
> the following parts of this discourse) how men, barely by
> the use of their natural faculties, may attain to all the
> knowledge they have, without the help of any innate im-
> pressions . . . (1.2.1.)

Here we see that Locke regards the issue between himself
and his opponent as one of producing the best theory to explain the facts of human knowledge. The opponent postulates 'certain innate principles' (Sometimes called 'innate
ideas') which are, in some sense, in the mind of man at the
moment of birth. Without these, he claims, we cannot fully
explain the facts in question.[6] Locke replies that he has a
better theory, empiricism, which will account for the facts in
a more satisfactory way. He is going to show how the facts
of human knowledge, in all their complexity and variety, can
be accounted for by sense-experience.[7]

[6] Such a view has recently been defended by Noam Chomsky in his *Cartesian Linguistics.*

[7] 'Whence comes [the mind] by that vast store which the busy and boundless
fancy of man has painted on it with an almost endless variety? Whence has it all
the materials of reason and knowledge? To this I answer, in one word, from
experience' (2.1.2). To show how this explanation works is the main task that
Locke sets himself in the *Essay.*

But the theories of Locke and his opponent cannot themselves be regarded as empirical statements. Locke is not saying that the existence or non-existence of innate ideas could be established by observation. His reason for rejecting them is that his own theory will provide a sufficient explanation. Again, when we turn to the details of that theory we find that it postulates certain processes which could hardly be regarded as matters of observation, for example the 'laying up of ideas' in the memory and a process of 'abstraction' whereby 'the mind' is supposed to form general concepts out of particular experiences. (See, e.g., 2.10.2, 2.11.9, 3.3.6.)

F. H. Bradley once observed that 'the man who is ready to prove that metaphysics is wholly impossible . . . is a brother metaphysician with a rival theory of first principles'.[8] The same may be said about Locke's theory of knowledge. Like other metaphysical doctrines, it tries to explain certain facts by appealing to 'first principles' which are beyond the reach of observation. Similarly, it has been held that by speaking of an unobservable entity, the soul, we can explain the differences between human beings and the rest of nature; that the regularities observable in the world are explicable by reference to a divine artificer; that the existence of general concepts requires a realm of 'universal' entities to explain it; and that there must be a world of 'real' things beyond experience, to explain the regularity of experience.

It appears, then, that scientific and metaphysical theories resemble one another both in going beyond observable facts and in providing, or aiming to provide, explanations of these facts. Sometimes, indeed, metaphysical views have been put forward in connection with scientific theories. An example is Einstein's remark 'God does not play dice'. Another is Newton's belief in forces behind the observable phenomena, which would explain them in some deeper sense than was achieved by his system of mechanics.

---

[8] F. H. Bradley, *Appearance and Reality*, p. 1. Compare Schlick's comment on the statement 'only the given exists' which he attributes to positivists of an older generation: 'Anyone who asserts this principle thereby attempts to advance a claim that is metaphysical in the same sense, and to the same degree, as the seemingly opposite contention, "There is a transcendent reality"' (previously quoted page 55).

But if the verificationist approach will not provide a means of eliminating the theories of metaphysics while retaining those of science, that does not mean that the question of verification is irrelevant when considering different kinds of theories and statements. This brings us to a question about what is to be included under 'verification'.

7.3 METHODS OF VERIFICATION

After affirming the connection of meaning with 'verification in experience' in one of his writings, Schlick added: 'The addition, "in experience", is really superfluous, as no other kind of verification has been defined' (*GA* p. 341, *PP* p. 458). Here Schlick has overlooked the kind of verification that is appropriate for *a priori* statements, for example those of logic and mathematics.[9]

It was sometimes denied by Logical Positivists that such statements are really statements. Schlick maintained that they were 'no proper "propositions" at all', but merely 'rules which determine the use of language' (*GA* pp. 145–6, *PP* p. 233). But this is a paradoxical way of marking the difference between *a priori* and empirical statements. Rules do not have a truth-value; but statements of logic and mathematics certainly do. A better way of marking the difference would be by reference to the different methods of verification. The verification principle is, indeed, well suited to bringing out the difference between the two types of statement: here is a difference of meaning which is faithfully reflected in the different methods of verification. I can verify that $99 \times 99 = 9801$ by a process of calculation, and this is very different from verifying that it is raining or that Caesar crossed the Rubicon. And this difference is a reflection of a difference in types of meaning. As Wittgenstein was to put it in the *Investigations,* the answer to the question about verification is 'a contribution to the grammar of the proposition'.[10]

[9] In speaking of 'experience', Schlick of course had in mind sense-experience, such as that of seeing. But A. C. Ewing pointed out that even this word can be used in a non-sensory way, as when we speak of seeing that one statement follows from another. ('Meaninglessness', *Mind* (1937).)

[10] Previously quoted on page 75.

Now philosophy too is an *a priori* discipline. Hence, if there are methods of verification in philosophy, we should not expect them to be of the empirical sort; and the same is true of metaphysical statements. When Ayer introduced his criterion in *Language, Truth and Logic,* he quoted a sentence from F. H. Bradley to illustrate the kind of metaphysical nonsense against which it would be effective: 'The Absolute enters into, but is itself incapable of, evolution and progress' (*LTL* p. 49). This, he said, was 'a remark taken at random' from Bradley's *Appearance and Reality.* Being 'not even in principle verifiable', it was nothing more than a 'metaphysical pseudo-proposition'.

If Ayer wanted a sentence that would strike the reader as meaningless, his example was well chosen. But does it seem so because it is unverifiable? Or does the trouble lie in the way it has been 'taken at random' out of its context? Perhaps if we read Bradley's book we shall find there the materials for assessing the truth of his statement. If the meaning of a statement is the method of its verification, then *that* is the sort of verification that must be sought in this case. What we must do, following the verification principle in this spirit, is to look to the philosopher's arguments to see what meaning (if any) his statements have; and this is certainly a sound principle. By contrast, to take such a statement 'at random' out of its context is simply to cut it off from the method of verification appropriate to it.[11]

The empiricist's answer to this will be to concede that there are two types of meaningful statements, but to insist that they are the only two. Bradley's statement, he will maintain, can be meaningful only if it is either empirical or analytic; reducible either to experiential statements or to statements derived from the meanings of words.

This dichotomy of statements has long been regarded by empiricists as essential to their view. As we saw on page 9, a similar principle was invoked by Hume in his raid on libraries in which there were works on 'divinity or school meta-

---

[11] Some of these points were made by Ayer himself in a later writing. See his editor's introduction to *Logical Positivism,* pp. 15–6.

physics'. It has not proved easy, however, to accommodate all meaningful statements within the dichotomy. The statements of mathematics are a notable example. Here we have a kind of statement whose truth-value can be proved *a priori,* without observation; but which is not analytic as is, say, the statement that a horse is an animal. The term 'analytic' was introduced by Kant, who spoke of the predicate term being 'contained in the concept' of the subject term.[12] Empiricists have generally thought that mathematics could be reduced to a kind of analytic discourse.[13] But even if this is so, it seems clear that there is a difference between it and analytic statements of the simple kind. For one thing, the possibility of error is different in the two cases. Someone who does not know that a horse is an animal would not be credited with knowing the meanings of these words; but one may easily be mistaken about the answer to '99 x 99' without being ignorant of the meanings of the words.

Perhaps, then, the *a priori* discourse of philosophy is of a different kind again, and not to be assimilated to other kinds. Leaving aside the case of Bradley's philosophy, let us consider this with regard to some methods of philosophy nearer to the Logical Positivists' own tradition.

7.4 METHODS OF PHILOSOPHY

When Locke tried to explain how we distinguish a memory-idea from an 'actual perception', he claimed that the former comes 'with a consciousness that it had been there before' and relied on the reader's introspection to bear this out.[14] Here we have a kind of philosophizing that is *a priori* in that it does not rely on sense-experience; but it is not *a priori* in

---

[12] Kant used the example 'All bodies are extended'. See his *Critique of Pure Reason,* A6–7. One of Kant's main contentions was that some truths are known *a priori* without being analytic.

[13] A notable exception was J. S. Mill, who regarded them as empirical. See his *System of Logic,* Book II, chs. V and VI.

[14] 'Whether this be not so, I appeal to everyone's observation' (*Essay,* 1.4.21). Locke thought of such observation as being done by a kind of 'internal sense'. See 2.1.2, 2.1.4.

the way of analysis or mathematics. Hume tells us how he cast about in his mind to see whether he could identify a 'self' as distinct from other items; and Descartes presented his 'method of doubt' as a kind of thought-experiment. Sometimes philosophers have used imagination as a criterion, drawing philosophical conclusions from facts about what is and is not imaginable.[15] It is true that many would regard such methods as irrelevant to philosophy, but the point is controversial and, in any case, the fact that they have been used remains.

But a more important method, from the point of view of our discussion, is that favoured by the Logical Empiricists themselves, namely analysis. The Logical Empiricists, as we saw, thought that they were on to a new conception of philosophy, one that would finally do away with the old problems. But the idea of analysis was not as new as one might have thought from the literature of the Vienna Circle. This was seen by Ayer, who claimed that anyone who read his own account and then turned to Locke's *Essay* could not 'fail to conclude that it is essentially an analytic work' (*LTL* p. 70). This is an over-simple view of the *Essay,* but there is some truth in it. Locke, and many other philosophers through the ages, can be described as trying to analyse certain concepts − such as those of substance, cause, identity, knowledge and virtue.

It is true that there was also something new about the Logical Empiricists' method of analysis. This was the truth-functional system of logic which had only recently been invented (and, later, the reduction-systems of Carnap). We have already seen that these systems are not as easy to apply as might have been thought. There is, however, another sort of difficulty about analysis, which has been more characteristic of philosophy through the ages. When philosophers have considered such concepts as those just mentioned, they have found it hard to agree on what are, and are not, essential features. Socrates, for example, disagreed with his friends about what is essential to such concepts as courage and piety.

[15] For a recent example, see P. F. Strawson's exposition of Kant, *The Bounds of Sense,* section 5.2.

Kant denied that emotion is part of the concept of morality; others have said that it is the most important part. Knowledge has been analysed as 'justified true belief', but this analysis has been the subject of much disagreement and revision.

The Logical Empiricists thought that with their new approach the old intractable questions would become plain and manageable.

> Neatness and clarity are our aim; we reject dark distances and unfathomable depths. In science there are no 'depths'; all is on the surface ... The scientific world-conception knows *no insoluble riddles* ... It is [the] *method of logical analysis* that essentially distinguishes the new empiricism and positivism from the old.[16]

But it is not clear how the old 'riddles' about morality, knowledge etc. could be disposed of either by the methods of science or by the mere application of a system of logic.

If knowledge is justified true belief, then, if Smith knows that *p,* he also believes that *p.* This is a logical truth, and can be set out as such in accordance with a logical system. But it is not philosophy. The philosophical question is, of course, whether to accept the first antecedent − the analysis of knowledge as justified true belief. How do I know whether this analysis is correct? I cannot get the answer merely by using a system of logic. The problem is not, or not merely, a problem of logic. If it were, then it could be solved by means of a computer. But philosophical problems are not solved by computers.

One thing I shall need to do to assess such an analysis is to consider how the word in question is used in ordinary contexts. The importance of considering ordinary uses of words was brought out by Wittgenstein in his later works. There is a passage in which he discussed a certain philosophical usage of 'know' and 'believe'. According to this, 'I can only *believe* that someone else is in pain, but I *know* it if I am'. Wittgenstein replied:

[16] 'The Scientific Conception of the World', *Erkenntnis* I, p. 15. Also see *Tractatus*, 6.5ff.

Yes: One can make the decision to say 'I believe he is in pain' instead of 'He is in pain'. But that is all. — What looks like a clarification here . . . is in truth an exchange of one expression for another which, while we are doing philosophy, seems the more appropriate one.[17]

Here we are dealing with another sort of analysis of 'knowledge' — one from which it would follow that 'I can only *believe* that someone else is in pain', etc. But this analysis is incompatible with the ordinary use of these words, and therefore it may be doubted whether the philosopher who speaks in these ways is any longer speaking about knowledge and belief. Perhaps the philosopher concerned would claim that his statement *is* in accordance with ordinary use (perhaps in some unobvious way that he could explain). If so, he would be contradicting Wittgenstein's observation in this case, but not the fundamental point about the importance of ordinary use.

This fundamental point was denied by Carnap when he wrote: 'A *philosophical* thesis on logic or language, in contrast to a psychological or linguistic thesis, is not intended to assert anything about the speaking or thinking habits of the majority of people, but rather something about possible kinds of meanings . . .'[18] Carnap thought that philosophy could be done by means of artificial languages, not owing allegiance to ordinary usage; and to the construction of such languages he devoted much thought throughout his life.

In view of Wittgenstein's argument it is not easy to see how this kind of enterprise could help us to understand the concepts, and answer the questions, that have troubled philosophers through the ages. But however this may be, the appeal to ordinary usage has in fact played a large role in the history of philosophy, at least since the time of Socrates. Here, however, we are dealing with questions which are neither metaphysical nor easy to accommodate within the

[17] *PI* 303. Wittgenstein also attacked the other part of the statement — the use of 'know' in reference to one's own pain. I have discussed this passage in my *Language and the Privacy of Experience*, sections 3.8 and 3.9.

[18] Schilpp (ed.), *The Philosophy of Rudolf Carnap*, p. 1003.

empirical/analytic dichotomy.[19] The facts in question are known — in a way — to any normal speaker of the language; but to make them explicit is very difficult and sometimes surprising. The fact that people use a given word, say 'knowledge', in the way they do, may seem at first sight an empirical one, of the same order as facts about the average rainfall. On this view one might think that questions about the uses of words must be answered by empirical methods, perhaps with the help of tape-recorders and computers. But it does not seem as if these methods could be either necessary or sufficient for the philosopher's purpose. On the one hand, being a normal speaker of the language, he already knows — in a way — how the words in question are used. On the other hand, to observe another person's use of them he would have to do more than merely record their sounds. He would need to enquire under what conditions this person deems it right to use the words, and why. And when these questions are pressed, they will lead precisely to the sort of difficulties that the philosopher himself had in trying to arrive at a satisfactory account. He will find himself in philosophical argument with the person questioned, following a method of philosophizing that found its classic expression in the Socratic dialogues.[20]

7.5 ELIMINATION AND THE VERIFICATION PRINCIPLE

The analytic/empirical dichotomy has nowhere been defended more stoutly than in the writings of verificationists. But what are we to say of the verification principle itself?

---

[19] For discussions of this problem see Colin Lyas (ed.), *Philosophy and Linguistics*.

[20] 'When we look for the most typical example of a philosophical mind we must direct our eyes towards Socrates. All the efforts of his acute mind and his fervent heart were devoted to the pursuit of meaning. He tried all his life to discover what it really was that men had in their minds when they discussed about virtue and the Good, about Justice and Piety; and his famous irony consisted in showing his disciples that even in their strongest assertions they did not know what they were talking about and that in their most ardent beliefs they hardly knew what they were believing.' (Schlick, *GA* p. 249, *PP* p. 369, *ER* p. 43.)

Does it fall within one class or the other? Or is it liable to eliminate itself as meaningless?

In Schlick's writings the principle seems at times to be viewed as a straightforward empirical truth. In 'Meaning and Verification' he spoke of it as 'nothing but a simple statement of the way in which meaning is *actually* assigned to propositions, both in everyday life and science' (*GA* p. 341, *PP* pp. 458–9). Ayer, on the other hand, said that his criterion of verifiability was to be regarded 'not as an empirical hypothesis, but as a definition' (*LTL* p. 21).

The verification principle could not be regarded as a principle or criterion if the empirical view were correct. To describe it merely as 'a statement of the way in which meaning is actually assigned' is to imply that meaning might conceivably have been assigned in another way. And this would mean that our concept of meaning is not necessarily connected with verification. Hence it would be wrong to regard verification as a criterion of meaning.

We would, however, be able to regard it thus if, following Ayer, we took the principle as 'a definition'. In that case we would hold that 'meaningful statement' may be *defined* as: 'statement which is either analytic or verifiable by observation'; and (turning to the verification principle as opposed to the criterion of verifiability) that 'meaning of a statement' may be defined as: 'method of verification of that statement'. If these or similar definitions are correct, then the verification principle and the criterion of verifiability will be analytic statements, and meaningful in the way that such statements are.

But are the definitions correct? The answer to this will depend on how the words in question are actually used. And as we saw in section 3.1, it does not appear that 'meaningful' and 'verifiable' are actually connected in the way required. (The difficulties of the verification principle were discussed in section 2.2.) Ayer was himself hesitant about his definition. The word 'meaning', he said, 'is commonly used in a variety of senses', and he wished only to claim 'that there was at least one proper use of the word "meaning"' which satisfied his definition (*LTL* p. 20). But later in the same paragraph he seemed to take a different view of his criterion, speaking of it now as a 'methodological principle'.

It has sometimes been held that a philosopher may need to revise, and not merely take note of, ordinary uses of words. According to Hempel, a philosopher should provide 'explications'.

> Explication is concerned with expressions whose meaning in conversational language or even in scientific discourse is more or less vague . . . and aims at giving those expressions a new and precisely determined meaning, so as to render them more suitable for a clear and rigorous discourse on the subject matter at hand . . . Taking its departure from the customary meanings of the terms, explication aims at reducing the limitations, ambiguities and inconsistencies of their ordinary usage by propounding a reinterpretation . . .[21]

Consider Russell's analysis of statements such as 'The present King of France is bald'.[22] Since there is no present King of France, one may well be in difficulties if asked whether the statement is true or false. Is it false? Neither true nor false? Meaningless? What, if any, are its logical relations with other statements? According to Russell, the statement may be analysed into several components, one being the assertion that there exists a present King of France. Analysed thus, the statement is simply and clearly false. The uncertainty of ordinary usage has been removed and the statement can take its place in relation to other true or false statements.

Another example may be taken from the writings of Carnap. Such statements as '*X* knows that the substance in this vessel is alcohol' should, according to Carnap, 'always be understood . . . in the sense of *imperfect knowledge,* that is, knowledge which has only a certain degree of assurance.[23] It

---

[21] *Fundamentals of Concept Formation in Empirical Science*, pp. 11ff.

[22] See 'The Philosophy of Logical Atomism', lecture VI, or *Introduction to Mathematical Philosophy*, ch. 16.

[23] 'Truth and Confirmation', in H. Feigl and W. Sellars, *Readings in Philosophical Analysis*, p. 120.

seems clear that this was intended as an improvement on, rather than a description of, ordinary usage.

Perhaps the verification principle, or the criterion of verifiability, can be regarded, in the same sort of way, as proposals for improvement or 'explications'. This was the view taken by Rynin, who thought of his own account, in 'Vindication of L*G*C*L P*S*T*V*SM', as a perfect example of Hempel's notion. Ayer, as we have seen, spoke of his criterion as a 'methodological principle'; and Carnap wrote that the 'Principle of Empiricism' should be put 'in the form of a proposal or requirement' (*TM* p. 84). Such a view has the immediate advantage of exempting the principle (or criterion) from self-application: a proposal is not something that is true or false and therefore there cannot be any question of verification.

About a proposal two questions may be asked: what are we asked to do, and why? Suppose I accept the criterion of verifiability in the sense of a proposal. What will this lead me to do? The answer may seem obvious: I shall, from now on, describe unverifiable statements as meaningless. But how can I describe them so if I don't believe them to be meaningless? Of course I could *say* 'meaningless', regardless of my belief. But what would be the point of this?

According to Hempel, the advantage of an 'explication' lies in rendering expressions 'more suitable for a clear and rigorous discourse' by removing the unclarities and ambiguities of ordinary language. Suppose I am given the task of writing a computer programme to work out logical relations between a number of statements. If Russell's sentence about the King of France is one of them, then I may find it difficult to proceed. Perhaps there is no provision for that kind of statement in the kind of programme I am writing. I may need to make a decision about the truth-values of such statements and this may lead me to use Russell's analysis. Here I would be replacing the uncertainty or ordinary language by 'a new and precisely determined meaning' in order to benefit from the clear and rigorous processes of the computer. This advantage, to be sure, would need to be balanced against a danger of misunderstanding. We would have to beware of confusing usefulness with truth; of assuming that to find an analysis useful is the same as discovering it to be true. And we must not lose sight of the distinction between the 'falseness' of Russell's example ('The present King of France is bald') and the straightforward *falseness* of such statements as 'The Prime Minister of England is bald'.

But what advantages, corresponding to those of Russell's analysis, could be claimed for the verification principle and criterion? The answer will depend on the success of the programmes of analysis discussed in chapters 4 and 6 — on whether they could result (as was intended) in a discourse that would be more 'clear and rigorous' than that of ordinary language. This was not the conclusion at which we arrived in those chapters.

There is, however, another sort of motive for accepting the principle, and especially the criterion, which makes them different from the case of Russell. The importance of this was seen by C. L. Stevenson in his 'Persuasive Definitions'.[24] Stevenson pointed out that sometimes, when a new definition is proposed, it is done in order to make something appear in a favourable or unfavourable light. One of his examples was the claim, made by some nineteenth-century critics, that Alexander Pope was not a poet. This, he said, followed from their definition of 'poet'; but the definition was itself motivated by an unfavourable attitude towards writers like Pope. A similar motive, said Stevenson, was at work in the verificationists' definition of 'meaning', and their application of this to metaphysics. They were, he said,

stating an unquestionable fact in their sense of meaning, just as the nineteenth-century critics were, in their sense of poet. The truth of such statements, however, is utterly beside the point. Controversy hinges on the emotive words that are used. Shall we define 'meaning' narrowly, so that science alone will receive this laudatory title, and metaphysics the correspondingly derogatory one of 'nonsense'? Shall our terminology show science in a fine light, and metaphysics in a poor one?

[24] *Mind* 1938; reprinted in Stevenson's *Facts and Values*.

But if 'the truth of such statements is utterly beside the point', why should we accept them? It is not enough to say that they follow from definitions that have been introduced; for this immediately raises the question why we should accept the definitions. Are they true definitions? If not, why should we accept them?

Stevenson went on to speak of reasons for accepting a new definition. The nineteenth-century critics, he said, 'were not condemning Pope with sheer bombast'.

Their narrow sense of 'poet' had the function of stressing, in the reader's attention, certain features common to most poetry, but lacking in Pope's. Perhaps they meant to say this: 'We have long been blind to fundamental differences between Pope's work and that of a Shakespeare or Milton. It is because of this blindness alone that we have been content to give Pope a laudatory title. Let us note the difference, then, and deprive him of the title.'

The claim of the Logical Positivists, thought Stevenson, would 'easily bear the same interpretation'.

Perhaps they meant to say: 'We have long been blind to the fundamental differences between the use of sentences in science and their use in metaphysics. It is because of this blindness that we have been content to dignify metaphysics with such titles as "meaningful". Let us define meaning, then, in a way that will at once stress these fundamental differences, and deprive metaphysics of its title.'

In these passages Stevenson draws attention to an important kind of controversy. When discussing whether something is a poem (a work of art, etc.), a clear line cannot be drawn between the question whether it satisfies existing criteria and the question what the criteria ought to be. (The same point may be made about such concepts as science, religion, democracy and philosophy itself.) In these arguments we stress certain features of the objects in question, relating them to other features, and to other objects of similar and contrasting

kinds. As a result we may come to have a different view of
the concept, finding it natural to include objects not included
before, or vice versa.

Now in Stevenson's examples two different considerations
are at work. One concerns the kind of argument just mentioned; and the other is about the 'laudatory' quality of such
words as 'poet'. Not every dispute about whether something
should be classified as an X has this laudatory aspect. But
where there is such an aspect, we may expect that the sitting
tenant, be he poet or metaphysician, will resist eviction.
There will be, moreover, no way of forcing him, and his
sympathizers, out. They must be *persuaded* that the accepted
description of him — as, say, a poet — is anomalous; that the
features in virtue of which he is so described are unimportant
compared to others. Perhaps, if they were shown that 'we
have long been blind to fundamental differences' between his
work and that of other poets, they would be prepared to
yield. (This will depend on what they think about the other
poets and, perhaps, on whether another laudatory description
is available in place of 'poet'.)

It is, however, not easy to see how such persuasion could
be brought to bear on the metaphysician and his audience. It
is true that the criterion of verifiability is meant to pick out a
fundamental difference among what we have been used to
regarding as statements; but this difference is hardly one to
which 'we have been blind'. On the contrary, we are well
aware that metaphysical statements are not, and not intended
to be, verifiable in the way that empirical statements are. On
the other hand, the evaluative connotation of 'meaningless'
is of a different order from that of 'poet'. To describe Pope's
works as 'not poetry' is not to deny them a place in literature. By contrast, to describe a set of statements as meaningless is to imply that they ought not to have been made. One
could hardly think it reasonable for those who make and
listen to metaphysical statements to accept this conclusion
merely by having pointed out to them something they knew
already. Hence it does not seem as if the   ʳᶦcationist's
claim can be represented, as Stevenson thought, as a shift of
definitions based on a new perception of fundamental differences.

7.6 *TRACTATUS*, VERIFICATIONISM, AND MEANING AS USE[25]

There is yet another way in which the verification principle might be regarded. After expounding the principle in his London lectures, Schlick continued:

> After you have once seen this clearly you will no longer understand even the possibility of a different opinion: you will recognize that no opinion can even be formulated without admitting the truth of the preceding remarks. The view contained in these remarks has, it is true, found many opponents, but the very name by which it is usually called shows that it has not been properly understood. It is known as the 'experimental theory of meaning'. But it is not a theory; there can be no theory of meaning. A theory is a set of hypotheses which may be either true or false and have to be tested by experience. It is not necessary to make hypotheses about meaning, and they would come too late, because we must presuppose meaning in order to formulate any hypotheses. We have not made any assumptions, we have done nothing but formulate the rules which everybody always follows whenever he tries to explain his own meaning and whenever he wants to understand other people's meaning, and which he never actually violates — except when he begins to philosophize.
> In establishing the identity of meaning and manner of verification we are not making any wonderful discovery, but are pointing to a mere truism. (*GA* pp. 181–2, *PP* p. 311, *ER* p. 34.)

In this passage Schlick may appear to be vacillating between the empirical and analytic views of the principle. He denies that it is 'to be tested by experience', and yet describes it as an account of something that 'everybody always' in fact

[25] An earlier version of this section has appeared in *Wittgenstein, the Vienna Circle and Critical Rationalism*, ed. H. Berghel.

does. And although he speaks of it as a 'mere truism', he does not seem to mean by this an analytic statement. But there are also echoes of Kant in the passage. According to Kant there are certain statements which, though not analytic, do not express empirical knowledge either. They express conditions which must be presupposed in order for such knowledge to be possible. The passage from Schlick contains a similar view of the verification principle. It is, he says, something whose truth must be admitted before any 'opinion can even be formulated'. Something must be presupposed in the formulation of 'any hypotheses': 'we must presuppose meaning'. He can hardly have meant by this merely that we must know what the hypotheses mean; what has to be presupposed, in Schlick's view, is that non-analytic non-theoretical 'truism', the verification principle.

It might be said, on this view, that the principle is not itself part of the language to which it is applicable. It is not subject to verification, because its truth is presupposed in saying anything whatever. It represents, so to speak, a point of view outside the whole of language, and therefore has a different status from either empirical or analytic statements.

Kant's view about a third class of statements went, of course, against the dichotomy to which empiricists have been committed; and there are frequent rejections of Kant in the writings of Logical Empiricists, including those of Schlick. Yet it seems as if, in this passage anyway, Schlick may have been influenced by Kant. But here, as elsewhere, it is likely that the more direct influence came from Wittgenstein. The view taken here of the verification principle might easily have been expressed in the language of the *Tractatus*. Thus it might have been said that the principle 'shows' itself, but is not 'said', in the language. Such a point had been made by Wittgenstein about what he called 'logical form'.

> Propositions can represent the whole of reality, but they cannot represent what they must have in common with reality in order to be able to represent it — logical form.
> In order to be able to represent logical form, we should have to be able to station ourselves with propositions somewhere outside logic . . .

Logical form, said Wittgenstein, is something that 'shows' itself in a proposition; and 'What *can* be shown, *cannot* be said.[26]

The contrast between saying and showing is now recognized to be one of the cardinal ideas of the *Tractatus*. It was, however, one that proved unacceptable to most members of the Vienna Circle.[27] In his *Logical Syntax of Language*, Carnap quoted at length from the *Tractatus* passage about saying and showing, and summed up: 'In other words: There are no sentences about the forms of sentences' (p. 282). This view he took to be refuted by what he had himself done in his book, which contained a great many 'sentences about the forms of sentences' — about the logical features of language, described by Carnap as its 'logical syntax'. But such a 'refutation' can be found also in the *Tractatus*; for it too contains many sentences about the forms of sentences. Nevertheless the account of language given in the *Tractatus* is such as to be inapplicable to that account itself. The propositions of the *Tractatus* do not themselves conform to the account of propositions expressed by them. That is what Wittgenstein meant in describing them as 'nonsensical'. They are a sort of ladder to a correct view of language and the world, which the reader must 'throw away . . . after he has climbed up it' (6.54).

Readers of the *Tractatus* have sometimes been bewildered by this conclusion. How can the author of a philosophical book tell us that what he has been saying all along cannot really be said? Some have regarded this part of the work as a regrettable lapse, due to a philosopher's addiction to paradox and not to be taken seriously. But there is no need to take this view. According to the *Tractatus*, the propositions of language have meaning by standing in a certain systematic relation to elements of the world. But if that is so, then the statement that they do so cannot itself have meaning in that way. The point can be brought out by reference to the

---

[26] *Tractatus* 4.12 – 4.1212.

[27] The story is told by Carnap in Schilpp (ed.), *The Philosophy of Rudolf Carnap*, pp. 28–9.

Tractatus 'picture theory' of meaning. According to this, the propositions of language are related to corresponding states of affairs in the world in the way that pictures are related to what they depict. Thus the proposition 'aRb' is a sort of picture of *a*'s standing in a certain relation to *b* — say that *a* is to the left of *b*. But the relation of depicting cannot itself be depicted. A picture showing *a* to the left of *b* together with the proposition 'aRb' (or any other picture showing a state of affairs together with a picture of it) would not depict the relation of depicting.

In a similar way the relation between name and object, as represented in the *Tractatus,* is not something that can be 'said'. In section 3.203 we read: 'A name means an object. The object is its meaning.' According to the *Tractatus,* language is composed of 'names', each of which is related to an 'object' by the relation of meaning; and every statement can be broken down into such names. But the statement about names and objects could not itself be broken down in that way; for what it speaks of, the relation between names and objects, is not itself an object — not an entity of the kind which, according to the statement, gives a name its meaning. Hence the statement lies outside its own definition of meaning.

Now as we saw in section 2.2, the view that one must go beyond language in order to account for the meaning of language was frequently stressed by Schlick, who saw the verification principle as an expression of it. He also, as we noted, conflated verification with ostensive definition. Schlick maintained that 'the discovery of the meaning of any proposition must ultimately be achieved by some act, some immediate procedure, for instance, as the showing of yellow' (*GA* p. 130, *PP* p. 220).[28] But the statement that all statements are ultimately definable by the ostensive method cannot itself be definable by that method. I may teach someone the meaning of 'yellow' by showing a sample of that colour; but I could not teach him the meaning of 'ostensive definition' in any such way. Hence, if it is true that all lan-

---

[28] Quoted above, page 19.

guage is based on ostensive definition, then this statement itself cannot be part of language.

Let us compare the *Tractatus* and verificationist views of meaning with those of the later Wittgenstein. The *Blue Book* opens with the question 'What is the meaning of a word?'. It does not, however, proceed to a direct answer. After pointing out that such questions give one a 'mental cramp', Wittgenstein wrote: 'We feel we can't point to anything in reply to them and yet ought to point to something.' After considering a number of approaches, Wittgenstein concluded: 'If we had to name anything which is the life of the sign, we should have to say that it was its *use*' (p. 4). In a later passage he wrote: 'The meaning of a phrase for us is characterized by the use we make of it' (p. 65).

In the *Tractatus,* and in the verification principle, the meaning of language is accounted for by something other than language; in the first case, a world that stands to language as a depicted situation stands to a picture of it; and in the second, an activity going beyond language. In the empiricism of Locke and others, a word has meaning by standing for a non-verbal mental entity, called an 'idea' (sometimes thought of as a mental image). Wittgenstein's 'use' is not another non-verbal item like these. The use of a word is not in that sense distinct from the word. If words did not exist, there would still be situations and activities; but this could not be said about a word and its use. Wittgenstein's claim about meaning and use is not a further attempt to answer the question 'What is language?' by reference to something other than language. It is a comprehensive rejection of such answers.

Is Wittgenstein's claim applicable to itself? Or does it, like the statements of the *Tractatus* and (on one view at least) the verification principle, fall outside its own description of language? There are grounds for answering each question in the affirmative.

Wittgenstein's claim has a negative and a positive aspect. He wished to deny in particular that meaning is, or is determined by, a mental process. It is possible to apply this claim to itself. What this would mean is that the meaning of the claim is not, and is not determined by, a mental process (such as a thought or mental image accompanying the utterance of it).

Wittgenstein's positive claim, on the other hand, is that to examine what a word means, we have to examine its use. To decide, for example, whether 'consciousness' means a mental process, we have to consider how the word is used.[29] Is Wittgenstein's positive claim applicable to itself? The claim is a claim about meaning. Applied to itself, it would be saying that to decide what 'meaning' means, we have to consider how this word is used. We might consider, for example, how we would use it in questions of the form 'When you said "X", did you mean Y?'[30]

Thus it appears that Wittgenstein's positive claim is also applicable to itself. There is, however, a sense in which it is not. Although we can, as just pointed out, consider how the word 'meaning' is itself used, we cannot regard this as a way of deciding the meaning of this word. For if someone rejects the claim about meaning and use, then it will be useless to ask him to consider the use of the word 'meaning'. He will regard this as relevant only if he *already accepts* the truth of the claim. Someone who accepts the truth of the claim will look to the uses of words to decide their meanings. He may also consider the use of the word 'meaning' itself. But he cannot regard this as a way of arriving at the meaning of 'meaning'.

[29] The question is discussed at *PI* 416ff.

[30] 'Someone says "Napoleon was crowned in 1804". I ask him "Did you mean the man who won the battle of Austerlitz?" He says "Yes, I meant him". – Does this mean that when he "meant him", he in some way thought of Napoleon's winning the battle of Austerlitz?' (*Blue and Brown Books*, p. 142).

8 The Accommodation of Ethics

8.1 ETHICS AS A SCIENCE

A main concern of the Logical Positivists, as we have seen, was to account for the various kinds of statements in a satisfactory way. Some attempts were also made to account for metaphysical statements, as distinct from merely describing them as meaningless. Carnap suggested that they serve to express an 'attitude to life' (*Lebensgefühl*), in the same sort of way as works of poetry or music. 'The metaphysician', he wrote, 'is a musician without musical ability'. Not having this ability, he expresses himself in the form of statements and theories; but really what he says is no more true or false than is a poem or a piece of music.[1] Ayer took a less tolerant line. 'The view that the metaphysician is to be reckoned among the poets appears to rest on the assumption that both talk nonsense.' This, he said, was unfair to poets (*LTL* p. 60).

But what was to be done about moral statements? A statement of the form 'X is good' may seem, on the face of it, to be of the same type as 'X is yellow'. G. E. Moore had maintained that ' "good" is a simple notion, just as "yellow" is a simple notion'; and that both words 'denote a simple and indefinable quality'.[2] On this view one might think that verificationists would treat 'good' as an observation-predicate, and 'X is good' as a statement to be analysed into hypothetical observation-statements. Yet it seems clear that 'good' is not an object of observation in the way in which, for

---

[1] 'The Elimination of Metaphysics', section 7 (trans. *LP*). Carnap suggested that the metaphysical doctrine of monism could find expression in the music of Mozart, while Beethoven was better suited to the rival doctrine of dualism.

[2] *Principia Ethica*, sections 7, 10.

example, 'yellow' is. Is it an object of observation in any sense? Ayer considered the view 'that statements of value are not controlled by observation, as ordinary empirical propositions are, but only by a mysterious "intellectual intuition" '. To this he objected that it would make statements of value unverifiable. 'For it is notorious that what seems intuitively certain to one person may seem doubtful, or even false, to another' (*LTL* pp. 140–1).

How then were statements of value to be accounted for? Being neither analytic nor, as it appears, empirical, must they not be classed with metaphysics? Such had been Carnap's view in his *Philosophy and Logical Syntax*. Value judgments, he said there, have 'no theoretical sense. Therefore we assign them to the realm of metaphysics' (p. 26). There is, however, a difference between moral and metaphysical discourse, which is ignored by this assimilation. Moral discourse is unavoidable, in a way in which metaphysical discourse is not. The verificationist critique, or some other, may convince us that metaphysical questions are meaningless; and as a result we may cease to ask them. But this could not happen with moral questions. For to a large extent moral questions are questions about what is to be done. I can ignore questions of metaphysics, astronomy or history, if I consider these subjects unimportant, uninteresting or meaningless. But I cannot take this attitude to moral questions. Faced with a moral choice between two actions, I have to decide one way or the other. Here is a question that demands an answer and cannot be set aside as meaningless.

Ethics was a relatively neglected topic in the Logical Positivists' writings. Carnap, their most prolific author, said hardly anything on the subject.[3] To a large extent the treatment of ethics was left to the moral philosopher C. L. Stevenson, who published a series of influential papers from 1937 onwards and whose book *Ethics and Language* appeared in 1944. It is true that Stevenson was not a Logical Positivist; as

---

[3]He came, in fact, to adopt a version of the 'emotivist' view, to be discussed below. See his 'Replies to critics' in Schilpp (ed.), *The Philosophy of Rudolf Carnap*, pp. 999ff. Such a view was also defended by Hans Reichenbach in *The Rise of Scientific Philosophy*, ch. 17, and by Ayer in *LTL* ch. 6.

we saw on page 141, he criticized the criterion of verifiability as a 'persuasive definition'.[4] Nevertheless his account of moral language has generally been favoured by supporters of Logical Positivism.

On the other hand, Schlick had published a book on ethics in 1930.[5] But when he came to write his later papers on meaning and knowledge (discussed in previous chapters), he seems to have lost his interest in the subject. Moreover, little was done to resolve the sharp difference which apparently existed between Schlick's book and the views of Stevenson, Ayer and others. According to the latter, moral statements are used to express feelings, attitudes or imperatives, rather than knowledge. Schlick, by contrast, had opened his book with the heading 'Ethics seeks nothing but knowledge'. Let us begin with a discussion of Schlick's view.

'If there are ethical questions which have meaning, and are therefore capable of being answered, then ethics is a science.' So runs the first sentence of Schlick's book. He went on to maintain that ethical questions are indeed meaningful and capable of being answered and that, accordingly, ethics is a science. Schlick saw his task as falling into two parts. The first, easy part, requiring no 'profound philosophical analysis', was to describe how words like 'good' are in fact used (*PE* p. 9). They are used, according to Schlick, to express desires; and these he regarded as facts of psychology.[6] The second part was the more important: 'here lies the proper task of ethics'. This was to examine the causal processes, social and psychological, which would explain, in a scientific way, why human beings have the desires that they have.

[4] Stevenson's view of meaning was a 'causal' one. He maintained that the meaning of a piece of language consists in its tendency to cause in the hearer a 'response' consisting of psychological processes. Seè *EL* p. 54.

[5] *Fragen der Ethik.* A translation by David Rynin, under the title *Problems of Ethics,* was published in 1939.

[6] As so often with Schlick's writings, it is not easy to ascertain what exactly his view is. In one passage he says that in calling an action good, 'I express the fact that I *desire* it' (*PE* p. 12); elsewhere he writes: 'moral precepts are nothing but the expressions of the desires of human society (*PE* p. 85); 'that is *called* good which is *believed* to bring the greatest happiness' (*PE* p. 87); and ' "I ought to do something" never means anything but "Someone wants me to do it." ' (*PE* p. 110).

The first part of Schlick's enquiry, asking us to consider how the word 'good' is 'actually used', is a remarkable anticipation of Wittgenstein's later methodology. The philosopher's task, maintained Schlick, is to describe and not to justify; to tell us 'what "good" *actually* means; he can never tell us what "good" *must* or *should* mean' (*PE* p. 18). This contrast between description and justification was fundamental to the later Wittgenstein's thought. The philosopher, he insisted, is to '*accept* the everyday language-game, and to note *false* accounts of the matter *as* false. The primitive language-game which children are taught needs no justification . . .' (*PI* p. 200). Wittgenstein wrote virtually nothing on ethics in his later period, but one might think that if he had written a book on the subject, his approach would have been very similar to Schlick's.[7]

This impression is not confirmed, however, if we turn to Wittgenstein's Lecture on Ethics, composed at about the same time as Schlick's book.[8] At least Wittgenstein would not have been happy with the idea of treating ethics as a science. For in his lecture he insisted that ethical judgments come *after* all the relevant scientific facts, including those of psychology, have been given. He spoke of 'absolute judgments of value', contrasting them with judgments which are relative to human desires. Someone who was playing tennis badly might, he said, explain himself by saying that he didn't desire to play well, and this would be acceptable. But it would be different if he were rebuked for telling a lie. If he said 'I know I behave badly, but then I don't want to behave any better', could the other person reply 'Ah, then that's all right'? 'Certainly not; he would say, "Well, you *ought* to want to behave better."' ('Lecture on Ethics', p. 5).

Schlick might try to account for this kind of statement by claiming that it too is derived from desires, in this case the desires of society rather than the individual. But that would

[7] In a passage in the *Investigations* he advises the reader to ask himself: 'How did we *learn* the meaning of this word ("good" for instance)? From what sort of examples? In what language-games?' (*PI* 77).

[8] Wittgenstein's lecture, prepared in 1929 or 1930, was published in 1965 in *The Philosophical Review*. Also see Wittgenstein's remarks on ethics, including those he wrote in his copy of Schlick's book, in *WWK* pp. 115–7.

only be putting the problem back a stage. For it is also possible to pass moral judgment on the desires of one's society,
adopting a standpoint that is outside existing desires.

In his book Schlick did not refer to Wittgenstein, but discussed the views of Mill and Kant. He considered Mill's
attempt 'to deduce from the fact that a thing was desired,
that it was in itself desirable' (p. 18).[9] Mill's critics, he said,
had accused him of confusing two meanings of 'desirable' −
'capable of being desired' and 'worth desiring' − only the
first of which followed from his premise. But, said Schlick,
what was wrong with the second meaning ('worth desiring' −
or as he put it, 'in itself desirable') was not that it did not
follow, but that it was no meaning at all.

> If I say of a thing that it is desirable, and mean that one
> must desire it as a means if one desires a certain end, then
> everything is perfectly clear. If, however, I assert that a
> thing is desirable simply in itself, I cannot say what I mean
> by this statement; it is not verifiable and is therefore
> meaningless. (*PE* p. 19.)

In another passage he said that to speak of an 'absolute'
moral judgment was like forgetting that 'the concept "uncle"
is defined relative to nephews and nieces' and that to speak
of 'an "absolute uncle" would be nonsense' (*PE* p. 112).

There is no place, in Schlick's account of moral discourse,
for the man who says 'I believe that X is wrong − in spite of
the fact that I desire it' (or '. . . in spite of the fact that X is
generally desired in my society'; or '. . . in spite of the fact
that X is likely to produce the greater amount of happiness').
According to Schlick, such a man must be contradicting himself. Kant, on the other hand, had maintained, not only that
such judgments were possible, but that a moral judgment is
essentially one that is independent of human desires. The
refutation of Kant's view was one of the main aims of
Schlick's book.[10]

[9] For Mill's deduction, see J. S. Mill, *Utilitarianism*, ch. 4.

[10] He accused Kant of the 'uncle' fallacy and concluded the book with a parody
of the 'hymn to duty' which appears in Kant's *Critique of Practical Reason*,
1.1.3 (*PE* p. 154).

Now as we have seen, Schlick based his enquiry on the facts of actual usage. Reflection on the actual use of a word like 'good' would show, he maintained, that moral judgments were nothing other than statements of empirical fact, in this case facts of human desire.

Discussing what he called 'the "Absolute Ought"', he accused Kant of not being sufficiently respectful of ordinary usage. 'He could not bring himself to leave its empirical meaning to this word, in which alone it is actually used. Everyone knows this meaning: "I ought to do something" never means anything but "Someone wants me to do it."' (*PE* p. 110). But Kant was not unmindful of ordinary usage. The question of what is 'pure morality' had, he said, been decided long ago by 'common sense' and 'ordinary usage'. A ten-year-old boy would show a grasp of it, and only philosophers and 'subtle reasoners' could put the matter into doubt.[11]

The difference between Schlick and Kant was not that one respected actual usage while the other did not; their disagreement was about the correct description of that usage. According to Kant, reflection would show that we have a concept of morality (or 'duty') as being independent of desires. (He referred to this independence as 'autonomy'.) Now it is true that many readers of Kant have objected to his sharp separation of 'pure morality' from the facts of desires and happiness. They would say that these facts have a place as reasons for moral judgments. But Kant has at least identified an essential aspect of the concept of morality. Not all moral questions can be answered, or fully answered, by reference to desires and happiness. A person may say that he ought to keep his promise even if this goes against his desires, and even though it may not promote the happiness of society or of anyone. His reason for saying that he ought to do X will be *that he promised* to do it. Again, a person may describe a practice Y as wrong even though Y is what most people desire to do.

These are facts about the usage of moral language, even if

---

[11] *Critique of Practical Reason,* part 2 (pp. 277, 273). Also see the *Groundwork,* ch. 2 (pp. 33–4).

they conflict with the verification principle. But do they? This would hardly be a suitable way of representing Kant's view. For Kant was concerned, above all, to show that moral judgments are based on reason. His view was not that they are not verifiable, but that their verification was of a very special kind, being neither scientific nor analytic. Their logical character was, he believed, such as to place them outside this dichotomy.[12] Kant's views cannot be examined here, but enough has been said to show that he was no advocate of the 'unity of science'. Whereas Schlick saw 'a happy simplification of the world-picture' (p. 30) in his assimilation of moral to scientific discourse, Kant was concerned to bring out the difference between them.[13]

8.2 ARE THERE MORAL FACTS?

As has been pointed out, Schlick's view of ethics was not that of the majority of Logical Positivists. They did not regard ethics as part of science or ethical statements as subject to verification. Their view was that such statements are non-cognitive — not expressive of knowledge, but of a person's feelings or attitudes. A contrast was made between facts and values; and between language that is descriptive and language that is prescriptive, imperative or emotive. On this view it makes no sense to speak of verifying a moral statement, any more than to speak of verifying an imperative, a question or a greeting. The verification principle was not intended for such speech-acts as these — though no doubt a verificationist will need to consider how their meanings are related to speech-acts that are verifiable.

The view that moral statements are non-cognitive is very widely accepted. It is often thought, in ordinary discussions,

[12] See the quotation from Kant, footnote 21, on page 122.

[13] On the same page Schlick declared that for the 'true philosopher' there is, *'sub specie aeternitatis* . . . only *one* reality and *one* science'. However, this enthusiasm for the unity of science was not maintained in some of his later writings. In 'L'école de Vienne et la Philosophie traditionelle' (1937), he criticized 'some of his friends' for thinking that philosophy could be replaced by science. (*GA* pp. 394–5.)

that merely to identify a question as moral is enough to show that it cannot be treated as one of fact, but must be left to the feelings of the individual. It is not easy, however, to produce arguments for this view. Sometimes it is thought enough merely to point out that moral statements are evaluative or expressive of attitudes, that they can be used with prescriptive force and so on. But an opponent of non-cognitivism need not (indeed, should not) deny these points. He may admit, for example, that the statement 'You ought to do X' is a way of telling someone to do X. His claim, however, will be that the statement can also be an expression of knowledge or belief, and capable of being true or false. These aspects are not incompatible, either in moral discourse or elsewhere.[14]

The non-cognitivist view is not supported by actual uses of the relevant words; for words like 'know', 'believe' and 'true' are commonly applied to moral statements. In response to the moral statement 'He was right to do X' one may say 'That's true'; whereas this would not make sense in response to the imperative 'Do X'. We also use the words 'know', 'true' etc. in contrasting morality with personal preference, as when we say 'I know I ought to do X, but I don't want to'.

Some of these points were recognized by A. J. Ayer in a paper published in 1949, in which he reconsidered the non-cognitivist account that he had put forward in *Language, Truth and Logic*. He now admitted that the view

which I still wish to hold, that what are called ethical statements are not really statements at all, that they are not descriptive of anything, that they cannot be either true or false, is in an obvious sense incorrect. For, as the English language is currently used — and what else, it may be asked, is here in question? — it is by no means improper to refer to ethical utterances as statements; when someone characterizes an action by the use of an ethical predicate, it is quite good usage to say that he is thereby describing

---

[14] 'Just as one can *warn* either by a command "Watch out for the bull" or by an assertion "There's a bull in that field", or advise by an imperative "Don't take that job" or a subjunctive "I wouldn't take that job if I were you", so one can prescribe conduct either by saying "Don't do it" or by saying "You ought not to do it" or "That would be an evil thing to do."'. (Alan R. White, *Truth*, p. 62.)

it; when someone wishes to assent to an ethical verdict, it is perfectly legitimate for him to say that it is true, or that it is a fact . . .

Nevertheless, continued Ayer, 'when one considers how these ethical statements are actually used, it may be found that they function so very differently from other types of statements that it is advisable to put them into a separate category altogether . . .'. Yet, after all, 'if someone still wishes to say that ethical statements are statements of fact, only it is a queer sort of fact, he is welcome to do so' (*Philosophical Essays,* pp. 231–3).

It may be thought that with these remarks, coming at the start of his paper, Ayer has given away his case before he has even stated it. Nevertheless he does his best to demonstrate the 'queerness' of moral facts, in the hope that the reader will, like himself, prefer to view them as not really facts at all, and moral statements as not really statements at all.

The reader is asked to suppose that someone had committed a murder, and to consider the various questions, physical and psychological, and including the wider circumstances, that might be asked about the deed. In getting answers to these questions, he would be getting the facts of the story; and these facts, said Ayer,

> are verified or confuted, as the case may be, by observation. It is a matter of fact, in my usage of the term, that the victim was killed at such and such a place and at such and such a time and in such and such a manner. It is also a matter of fact that the murderer had certain . . . motives. (*Philosophical Essays,* p. 234.)

But suppose we now raised a question of right or wrong (assuming, say, that the killer had some justification for his deed). In getting an answer to this question, would we be getting more of the facts of the story? No, answers Ayer.

> To say that his motives were good, or that they were bad, is not to say what they were. To say that the man acted rightly, or that he acted wrongly, is not to say what he did.

And when one has said what he did, when one has described the situation in the way I have outlined, then to
add that he was justified, or alternatively that he was not,
is not to say any more about what he did; it does not add a
further detail to the story. (P. 235.)

There is, undoubtedly, something right about Ayer's
claims. To begin with, one could hardly disagree with what
he says in the first two sentences. But to this it may be replied that what he says there is beside the point. To describe
the motives as good or bad is not, indeed, to say what they
were; and likewise in the case of describing the action as right
or wrong. Nevertheless, it may be said, one would be *describing* the motives and the action. Ayer himself had pointed out
(as we saw) that it would be 'quite good usage' to speak of
this as describing. What he needs to show is that this usage —
with its 'factual' implications — should be discontinued.

Again, Ayer is right to say that in adding a moral predicate
one would not be adding 'a further detail to the story'. Someone giving a report of the incident would be making a curious
mistake if he thought that the moral statement should be included with the details of where, when and how. But the
reason for this, it may be replied, is not that the moral statement is not a statement of fact; it is, rather, that this fact is
not a *detail*. The statement that the action was right or wrong
(as the case may be) is a statement about the incident as a
whole; it is made after considering all the details and is not,
therefore, one of them.

But what, we may ask, is the relation between the details
and the moral conclusion? Ayer admitted that we give
reasons for our moral statements, and the details of the case
would obviously be among these. But, he continued, 'the
question is: In what way do these reasons support the [moral]
judgments? Not in a logical sense. Ethical argument is not
formal demonstration' (*Philosophical Essays,* p. 236). If the
moral judgment followed logically from the reasons, then one
could hardly deny that it can be an object of belief and
knowledge, no less than the reasons. But according to Ayer,
there is no logical connection.

In the passage just quoted, Ayer takes it for granted that

'logical' must mean 'by formal demonstration'. But this is a mistake. There is a logical connection between 'causing unnecessary harm to others' and 'wrong', but it is not one of formal demonstration. Someone who described such an action as good might be said to be contradicting himself, but it would not be a formal contradiction as would, for example, the description of a horse as a vegetable, which can be analysed into a conjunction of p and not-p. Again, there is a logical connection between 'He promised to do X' and 'He ought to do X', but someone who affirmed the first while denying the second would not necessarily be contradicting himself. There is also a logical connection between 'Smith has been insulted' and 'Smith is angry', but, once more, it is not a matter of formal demonstration or self-contradiction. In each of these cases, however, it is a matter of logic that the truth of one statement is a reason for believing in the truth of the other — even though any particular inference will depend on circumstances.

Locke, in his discussion of moral concepts, had perhaps been nearer to the truth than Ayer. He spoke of 'moral knowledge', which he attributed to 'the contemplation of our own *moral ideas*'. 'Let a man have the *idea* of taking from others, without their consent, what their honest industry has possessed them of, and call this *justice* if he please.' Such a man, argued Locke, could not be using the word 'justice' in its normal sense (*Essay,* 4.4.9.).

It seems, however, that Ayer had in mind the kind of moral situation, familiar enough, in which it is hard to come down on one side or the other. In his story he asks the reader to assume 'that two observers agree about all the circumstances of the case . . . but that they disagree in their evaluation of it'. In that case, he claimed, 'neither is contradicting himself' (*Philosophical Essays,* p. 236). It is certainly true that there are cases in which two people may disagree in their moral evaluations, without falling under the suspicion of not using words in their normal senses. This is also true of some questions of principle as opposed to particular cases. Thus people may reasonably disagree about the rights and wrongs of pornography, euthanasia and capital punishment. But there are also moral truths where this is not so. Such is the wrongness of causing unnecessary harm and the obligation, other things being equal, to keep one's promises.

It is easy to overlook the existence of examples of the second kind, just because they are not issues for discussion. They belong to the bedrock of rationality, to the beliefs and attitudes that are taken for granted by any normal person. If, however, we confine our attention to cases of the contentious kind, then we may easily conclude that moral questions are essentially inconclusive and that therefore the concepts of fact, knowledge and truth have no place in morality.

It may be thought that the existence of contentious cases is peculiar to morality, and that this somehow casts doubt on the objectivity of moral facts in general — making them, as Ayer put it, 'a queer sort of fact'. It is not true, however, that contentious cases are peculiar to morality. We have already seen (section 4.7) that we may prefer to speak of a scientific theory as 'good' or 'satisfactory' rather than true or false. Thus we may say, paraphrasing Ayer's claim about the moral case, that two observers may agree about all the facts of a scientific enquiry and yet disagree in their theoretical accounts of them. Someone who accepted the facts on which Darwin's theory of evolution is based, and yet rejected the theory, would not be contradicting himself. Sometimes, of course, such questions are unresolved merely because our knowledge of the relevant facts is incomplete (just as it may be in moral cases). But that is not always the reason. Rival theories are not necessarily rival speculations about unobserved facts.

A similar point may be made about particular causal questions, both inside and outside science. Different historians, using the same data, may not be able to agree on what was the cause, or the main cause, of a given event.

Finally, there is a general way in which contentious cases arise in the uses of words. When is it correct to describe something as an *X*? It is generally held that the whale is not a fish but a mammal. But when Melville examined the matter in *Moby Dick*, he concluded — after considering all the relevant data — that the whale is a fish. Was he contradicting himself? It would not do to reply that 'by definition' the whale is not a fish, for Melville's argument is just that this definition is wrong. And if it is thought that the status of the whale is beyond dispute, the same is certainly not true of other questions of taxonomy. Nor is it true of the uses of words generally. Faced with the same data, we disagree with one another on whether X should be described as a religion, Y as a work of art or Z as an example of democracy. Even in the case of colour-words, where, as we may say, only one datum needs to be considered, there may be disagreement about the correct description. But in none of these examples, any more than in the case of moral discourse, does the existence of contentious cases mean that we cannot, in *other* examples of the same discourse, speak of knowledge and truth.

8.3 BELIEF AND ACTION, CAUSES AND REASONS

We have seen (page 159) that according to Ayer 'two observers may agree about all the circumstances of the case' while disagreeing 'in their evaluation of it', and yet neither would be 'contradicting himself'. In another passage he made a similar point about the logical relation between the two observers.

It is, indeed, true that in a case where one person A approves of X, and another person B approves of not-X, A may correctly express his attitude towards X by saying that it is good, or right, and that B may correctly use the same term to express his attitude towards not-X. But there is no contradiction here. (*Philosophical Essays*, p. 247.)

There is no contradiction because, according to Ayer, the description of X as right or wrong is merely an expression of personal preference. If one person says he likes bananas and another says he does not, there is no contradiction between them, for both statements may be true. It would be different if they disagreed about an objective quality of bananas, for example about their nutritive effects. But according to Ayer there cannot be objective disagreement in ethics — disagreement as to whether X is really right or wrong, as distinct from the preferences of individuals. Yet, when Moore had considered the matter many years earlier, he described as an 'absurdity' the view 'that no two men ever differ in opinion as to whether an action is right or wrong' (*Ethics*, OUP edn., p. 61).

Stevenson's treatment seems at first sight more satisfactory than that of Ayer. He did not deny that there would be a contradiction between two persons such as *A* and *B*; but in his view it would be a contradiction between imperatives and not opinions.

In the opening sections of *Ethics and Language,* Stevenson produced a set of 'working models' for the analysis of moral terms.

(1) 'This is wrong' means *I disapprove of this; do so as well.*
(2) 'He ought to do this' means *I disapprove of his leaving this undone; do so as well.*
(3) 'This is good' means *I approve of this; do so as well.* (*EL* p. 21.)

In subsequent discussions Stevenson tried to do justice to the complexities of ordinary language by showing how the components of his working models might appear in various guises and combinations; but it remained his view that they were the essential components.[15]

In each of Stevenson's models there is one component that is amenable to verification and another that is not. A statement such as 'I approve' may be true or false, and there are ways of verifying it. But this cannot be said about the second, imperative component. Stevenson put the matter as follows:

The model for 'This is good' consists of the conjunction of (a) 'I approve of this', and (b) 'Do so as well'. If a proof is

[15] In a later analysis, for example, Stevenson saw a need for 'recognizing rich and varied descriptive meanings for ethical terms, in addition to emotive meaning (section IX/1; see table of contents, p. x). But see his emphatic statement of the 'general point', that the complexities he has recognized make 'no essential difference', their existence making ethics 'neither richer nor poorer ... and neither more nor less "objective"' (*EL* p. 209).

possible for (a) and (b) taken separately, then and only then will it be possible for their conjunction. So let us see what can be done with the sentences separately.

Sentence (a) offers no trouble. It makes an assertion about the speaker's state of mind, and like any psychological statement, is open to confirmation or disconfirmation, whether introspective or behavioristic.

Sentence (b), however, raises a question. Since it is an imperative, it is not open to proof at all . . . (*EL* p. 26.)

It is component (b) of this analysis that represents the possibility of moral disagreement. According to Stevenson, such a disagreement consists, in effect, of A asking B to approve of X and B asking A to approve of not-X.

Stevenson recognized that his analysis would need some adaptation in dealing with the case in which one is not saying that X is good, but wondering whether it is. It is difficult to apply component (a) here, for a person in this position is not trying to discover (by introspection or otherwise) what his 'state of mind' is. The question he asks himself is not whether he already approves of X, but whether he ought to approve of it; whether X is (irrespective of his current state of mind) good or bad, right or wrong. His position is similar to that of someone considering a non-moral question. Such a person is not asking himself whether he already believes that p; his question is whether he *ought* to believe it — whether p is (irrespective of his current state of mind) true or false.

Stevenson thought, however, that component (b) could easily be adapted so as to account for the first-person case. In this case, he said, there is a 'conflict of attitudes' of the same kind as that which may exist between two persons. He spoke of this (quoting John Dewey) as a matter of incompatible desires and 'competing preferences' (*EL* pp. 130–1). But again, though it is true that a person may have incompatible desires, he will not be able to answer the question whether X is right or wrong merely by reflecting on his desires. Indeed, he may conclude that X is wrong in spite of the fact that he desires to do it more than anything else.

Stevenson's analysis may seem at first sight to work better for the interpersonal than for the personal case. But this is

not so; for the analysis is hardly coherent, even in the inter-
personal case. This is connected with the importance of
reasons, as distinct from imperatives and psychological facts.
The imperative 'do so as well', requesting approval, does not
make sense. A person can be requested to do something only
if it is possible for him to choose to do it; but this is not the
case with approval. If you tell me your reasons, I will *see
whether* I approve of X.[16] I cannot choose to approve of X,
any more than I can choose to believe that p; and in neither
case would it make sense to address an imperative to me. But
on the other hand, this part of Stevenson's analysis is redundant; for what he is trying to express by it is already there in
the first part. As we saw, Stevenson regarded this part ('I approve of this') as 'an assertion about the speaker's state of
mind'. But this is no more true of 'I approve' than of 'I
believe'.[17] If you say 'I approve of X' and I say 'I agree',
then what we agree about is not your state of mind; it is the
description of X as a good thing. On the other hand, if you
approve and I disapprove of X, then we do not merely differ
in our states of mind; we disagree about the correct description of X. Thus the possibility of disagreement is already
there in the use of 'I approve' and there is no need for
Stevenson to introduce his imperative in order to account for
it.

   This is not to deny that in saying 'I approve of X' (or 'I
believe that p') one is stating a fact about oneself. But this
fact cannot be regarded as a separate component, in the way
described by Stevenson. For the statement about oneself
makes no sense in isolation from the claim about X (or about
p). Here it is illuminating to consider the question 'Why?'.
Someone who says 'I approve of capital punishment' must be
prepared to deal with this question. The question is not, however, about his psychological or bodily state; it is about the
rightness of capital punishment. (A similar point was made in
section 6.2 about emotions.) Similarly, a person who expres-

[16] 'See whether' does not mean introspection, however. What I must decide is not
whether my 'state of mind' is one of approval, but whether it is *right* for me to
approve. This requires an examination of the reasons and not of my state of mind.

[17] See R. M. Hare, *The Language of Morals*, p. 6.

ses a belief that *p* must be prepared to deal with the question 'Why?'; and this again is not a question about his psychological or bodily state, but about the truth of *p*. What is wanted is a reason for approving of *X*, or believing that *p*, as opposed to information about the speaker's mind or body. This connection with reasons is essential to the meanings of 'I approve' and 'I believe'; there is no *separable* fact about the speaker that they can serve to convey.

This is not to say, of course, that one must always be able to give good reasons for one's belief. For one thing, the reasons may be less than good but still recognizable as reasons. But in some cases one may not need to be able to give reasons at all. This may be so, for example, in believing that the battle of Lepanto occurred in 1571, where one may have forgotten what led one to have the belief. Even here, however, one must be (as I put it) 'prepared to deal with' the question 'Why?'. In this case one may have to deal with it by explaining to the questioner why, in this case, the question 'Why?' does not have to be answered. But with other cases of belief something more is required. Asked why I believe that the company will make a profit (or again, why I approve of capital punishment) I cannot normally say that I have forgotten my reasons.

The parallels between 'I approve' and 'I believe' suggest that the difference between them is not as fundamental as it would appear from such writers as Stevenson and Ayer. In my discussion I have spoken of approval 'of *X*' and belief 'that *p*', but the difference between these forms can easily be eliminated. Thus instead of speaking of approval of *X* we can speak of a *belief that X* is right. And our reasons for approving of *X* will be, *ipso facto*, reasons for believing that *X* is right. In this way a person's moral views can be seen as beliefs, forming part of his system of beliefs.

Now as we saw on page 158, Ayer denied that the connection between 'the facts of the case' and the moral statement could be a logical one. Like Stevenson, he maintained that the connection could only be one of cause and effect. On this view, giving someone a reason for approving of *X* differs from giving him an aspirin to remove his headache only in so far as different laws of nature are involved. It is a general fact of human nature that we approve of honesty and disapprove of cruelty. Hence by informing someone of the facts of a case I can cause him to feel approval or disapproval, as the case may be. If my statements do not produce the desired result, I may try others; just as I may try a different tablet if the aspirin failed to work. It was important to Stevenson and Ayer to deny that the move from 'the facts of the case' to the moral conclusion could be a logical one, because if it were, then the latter must be a possible object of knowledge no less than the former. But this would not be so if the connection were causal as opposed to logical. Hearing the facts of the case may cause me, for example, to fall asleep. But falling asleep would not be a piece of knowledge deduced from the facts of the case.

Now it is true that moral reasoning can be described in causal terms (though it must be noted, again, that the same is true of non-moral reasoning). Thus instead of referring to certain facts as 'my reasons', I may speak of them as 'causing' my attitude (or belief). The notions of reason and cause are related, because both have to do with antecedent conditions; and the word 'because' is equally at home in both contexts — in 'I fell asleep because . . .' as well as in 'I approve of X because . . .'.

This assimilation is, however, deceptive. It is a widely accepted principle that there are no *a priori* restrictions on what may be the cause of a thing. 'To consider the matter *a priori*', wrote Hume, 'any thing may be the cause of any thing' (*Treatise,* p. 247). Could the same be said about reasons that are given for or against approval of X? According to Stevenson, it could.

> *Any* statement about *any* matter of fact which *any* speaker considers likely to alter attitudes may be adduced as a reason for or against an ethical judgment. Whether this reason will in fact support or oppose the judgment will depend on whether the hearer believes it, and upon whether, if he does, it will actually make a difference to his attitudes . . . (*EL* pp. 114–5.)

Now it is true that Hume's dictum is subject to qualifications. For one thing, Hume himself maintained that 'the cause must be prior to the effect' (*Treatise* p. 173). Nevertheless Hume is largely right in seeing the causal relation as a matter of empirical, and perhaps surprising, discovery. In this respect it differs, however, from the relation between attitudes and reasons for them. The difference can be brought out by making a point that is similar to Hume's dictum. We may know that two things are connected as cause and effect, without having the least idea *how* they are connected. In answer to the question 'Why do aspirins relieve pain?' one may answer 'I don't know' — or even 'Nobody knows'. It would still make sense, however, to claim that aspirins relieve pain — that they are a cause of relief. But this is not so in the case of 'adducing a reason for or against an ethical judgment'. Someone who 'adduces the reason' that it is raining today as a reason for approving of capital punishment cannot answer 'I don't know' when asked what the connection is. If we cannot see the connection, then we cannot say that he has adduced a reason. The same point applies to non-moral beliefs. In adducing a reason for my belief that the train will leave at 8.30, I must refer to something that is connected with my belief, not merely by way of cause and effect, but in such a way that the connection can be seen or explained. Giving a reason for one's belief, whether moral or non-moral, is different from a mere statement of cause and effect.

But the connections and parallels between moral and non-moral beliefs should not lead us to overlook the differences between them. One of these is that moral beliefs are 'practical' in a way in which others are not. If I have reason to believe that X is the right thing for me to do, then that very reason is a reason for me *to do X*. Now it is sometimes thought that just because of this connection with action, 'reason' cannot mean in the moral case what is means in the case of ordinary belief. For how can there be a logical progression in which the conclusion is an action? In reasoning from premises to a conclusion, we trace a relation between a number of truths. If the premises are true, and are connected in certain ways with the conclusion, then the latter will be true also. But an action (unlike a belief) cannot be described either as true or as false. Actions do not seem to be of the right type to enter into logical relations with statements or beliefs. Stevenson made the same point with regard to 'expressions of approval'.

> A man's willingness to say that X is good, and hence to express his approval, will depend partly on his beliefs . . . His reasons do not 'entail' his expression of approval, of course, or make it 'probable'. An expression of attitude cannot stand in these logical relationships to descriptive statements but only in causal relationships.[18]

Stevenson is right in saying that a descriptive statement cannot be said to 'entail' an expression of attitude. But, once again, the same point can be made about expressions of belief. A statement can be said to entail other statements; it cannot be said to entail happenings, such as the expression of a belief or an attitude. Nor can it be said to entail the *having* of a belief or attitude (as distinct from expressions of them).[19] 'This is a horse' entails 'This is an animal'; but it cannot be said to entail that anyone has, or has expressed, a belief or attitude about these statements or about anything else. This lack of entailment does not mean, however, that one cannot have reasons for a belief. My reason for believing that it has been raining is that the pavements are wet. But this does not mean that my belief is 'entailed by a descriptive statement' (or by anything else). Similarly, if my reason for approving of X is that X will make someone happy, the relation between reason and approval cannot be one of entailment (nor, as I have argued, is it one of cause and effect). If the reasonableness of beliefs or attitudes depended on their being entailed by descriptive statements (or by anything else), then neither beliefs nor attitudes could ever be reason-

---

[18] *Facts and Values* p. 67. Compare Hume's claim that ''tis not contrary to reason to prefer the destruction of the whole world to the scratching of my finger' (*Treatise*, p. 416).

[19] Aristotle was right in seeing an analogy between reasoning that results in a belief and reasoning that results in an action (the 'practical syllogism'). In the former, he said, 'the mind is forced to *affirm* the conclusion'; in the latter 'we are forced straightway to *do* it' (*Nichomachean Ethics*, 7.3.4). In both cases (affirmation, action) the result is not something that follows from the premises by entailment.

able. This is not however, what is meant by 'reasonable' and 'having a reason'.[20]

It remains true, however, that there is a kind of relation among beliefs which cannot obtain between beliefs and actions. Beliefs resemble statements in being true or false, and this is not so with actions. But this does not mean that there are no logical relations between beliefs and actions; it means that they are different from those between beliefs and beliefs (which again are different from those between statements and statements, where we may speak of entailment). One's action may be inconsistent with one's belief; but though this inconsistency is logical, it differs in certain ways from that which may exist between beliefs (or between statements). Finally, this point again applies to non-moral as well as moral beliefs. As we saw in section 2.3, there is a logical connection between 'It is raining' and such actions as taking an umbrella. In this case too, an action may be consistent or inconsistent with one's belief.

Moral statements, it was pointed out at the start of this chapter, presented themselves to the verificationists as needing to be accounted for in accordance with their principle. What becomes of this problem if the non-cognitivist view is rejected? One might think that, either way, there should not be any special problem about moral statements. If it is true that they are really (say) imperatives, then the question of verification cannot arise. If, on the other hand, they are expressions of belief and knowledge, capable of being supported by reasons, then they should be verifiable just as much as other statements. If having promised to do something is a reason for doing it, then the statement 'He ought to do X' can be verified by an observation that he promised to do X. (It is true that the observation will not strictly entail the truth of the statement, but the same may be said about non-moral statements, as we saw in section 4.2.)

The difficulty about moral statements, from the point of view of a verificationist, is not that they are not verifiable, but that the connection with action is particularly marked in their case. This applies especially to statements like 'He ought

---

[20] See Roy Edgley, *Reason in Theory and Practice*, pp. 104–5.

to do *X*'. To understand this requires an understanding of
what he ought to do, and this is different from understanding
a method of verification (though the latter will be relevant
too). The verification principle is particularly inadequate in
accounting for the practical aspects of language.

There also remains a problem about contentious cases. On
page 160 I made the point that these are sometimes given
undue prominence in discussions of moral discourse. But
they should not be overlooked either. In their case we would
not speak of verification or knowledge, and to that extent
the non-cognitivist view is right. But we would, contrary to
that view, speak of *reasons* (in this case conflicting reasons)
for regarding *X* as right or wrong. And we might also say,
adapting the verification principle, that to understand such a
problem requires an understanding of the relevant reasons.
But it would be wrong, in this case, to regard reasons as
methods of verification.

9 Conclusion

The conclusions arrived at in this book have been to a large extent negative. All sorts of objections and difficulties have presented themselves in our examination of the views in question. These results will not surprise anyone who is familiar with the critical literature about Logical Positivism, which has appeared since the early days of the movement. But, on the other hand, it is not a result that is peculiar to Logical Positivism; for, again, anyone familiar with discussions of past philosophers in general will know that they consist to a large extent of objections and difficulties. That this is so does not, however, constitute a sufficient reason for losing interest in these philosophers. Perhaps what is peculiar to Logical Positivism, and what led to the view, referred to in my opening pages, that it is 'a dead horse', is the swiftness and forcefulness of the critical literature in its case.

In my Introduction I quoted a typical passage from Carnap, in which he expressed astonishment that 'so many men . . . outstanding minds among them, have devoted so much effort, and indeed fervour, to metaphysics, when this consists in nothing more than words strung together without sense'. After reading the critical literature about Logical Positivism, one may be tempted to express a similar astonishment about the men who devoted so much effort and fervour to the construction and exposition of that philosophy. It can hardly be denied, moreover, that these men too had some outstanding minds among them. And the same may be said of the many readers, both inside and outside the ranks of philosophers, who have felt themselves attracted by the new philosophy. It is likely, indeed, that the forcefulness of the critical literature was provoked by the widespread success of the new ideas.

The Logical Positivists and their sympathetic readers were not fools; and the fact that their ideas are exposed to serious objections does not prove that they were. The importance of a philosophical movement does not lie in immunity from objections, but from an ability to arouse the interest and critical reaction of those who think about the fundamental

171

questions of philosophy. The Logical Positivists did not only deal with such questions; they were also responsible for a new appreciation of the importance of some of them. This is especially true of questions about meaning. What they had to say about these questions was, as I have said, open to a variety of objections; but, as I have tried to show in the book, there was usually some truth in it. In any case, the Logical Positivist approach (like the more general empiricist approach) will, I believe, always suggest itself as an option to be considered by those who think seriously about the problems of philosophy. If this is so, then Logical Positivism can take its place among the philosophers and philosophical movements which are of lasting importance.

BIBLIOGRAPHY

Achinstein, P. 'The Problem of Theoretical Terms', *American Philosophical Quarterly* (1965).

Ayer, A. J. *Language, Truth and Logic,* 1936; Penguin, 1971.

The Foundation of Empirical Knowledge, Macmillan, 1940.

(ed.) *Logical Positivism,* Allen & Unwin, 1959.

Philosophical Essays, Macmillan, 1965.

Part of my Life, OUP, 1978.

Berkeley, G. *The Principles of Human Knowledge,* 1710.

Berghel, M. (ed.) *Wittgenstein, the Vienna Circle and Critical Rationalism,* Reidel, 1979.

Bradley, F. H. *Appearance and Reality,* OUP, 1893.

Bridgman, P. W. *The Logic of Modern Physics,* Macmillan, 1927.

Brown, R. and Watling, J. 'Amending the Verification Principle' in *Analysis* (1950–51).

Carnap, R. *Der Logische Aufbau der Welt,* 1928; F. Meiner, 1962.

'Die alte und die neue Logik', in *Erkenntnis* I (1930–31).

'Überwindung der Metaphysik durch logische Analyse der Sprache', in *Erkenntnis* II (1931).

'Psychologie in physikalischer Sprache', in *Erkenntnis* II (1931).

'Über Protokollsätze', in *Erkenntnis* III (1932–31).

The Unity of Science, trans. M. Black, Kegan Paul, 1934.

Philosophy and Logical Syntax, Kegan Paul, 1935.

The Logical Syntax of Language, trans. A. Smeaton, Routledge, 1937.

'Testability and Meaning' in H. Feigl and M. Brodbeck (eds.), *Readings in the Philosophy of Science,* Appleton, 1953.

The Philosophy of Rudolf Carnap, ed. P. A. Schilpp, Open Court, 1963.

Church, A. Review of Ayer's *Language, Truth and Logic,* in *Journal of Symbolic Logic,* vol. 14 (1949).

Dummett, M. *Frege,* Duckworth, 1973.

Edgley, R. *Reason in Theory and Practice,* Hutchinson, 1969.

Edwards, P. and Pap, A. (eds.) *A Modern Introduction to Philosophy,* Collier, 1965.

Edwards, P. (ed.) *Encyclopedia of Philosophy,* Collier–Macmillan, 1972.

Evans, J. L. 'On Meaning and Verification', in *Mind* (1953).

Ewing, A. C. 'Meaninglessness', *Mind* (1937).

Feigl, H. (ed.) *Minnesota Studies in the Philosophy of Science,* vol. 1, Minnesota UP, 1956.

Feigl, H. and Brodbeck, M. (eds.) *Readings in the Philosophy of Science,* Appleton, 1953.

Feigl, H. and Sellars, W. (eds.) *Readings in Philosophical Analysis,* Appleton, 1949.

Frege, G. *Foundation of Arithmetic,* trans. J. L. Austin, Blackwell, 1953.

Hanfling, O. *Language and the Privacy of Experience,* Open University, 1976.

'Does Language Need Rules?', in *Philosophical Quarterly* (1980).

(ed.) *Essential Readings in Logical Positivism,* Blackwell, 1981.

Hempel, C. 'Some Remarks on "Facts" and Propositions', *Analysis* (1935).

'On the Logical Positivists' Theory of Truth', *Analysis* (1935).

Fundamentals of Concept Formation in Empirical Science, University of Chicago, 1952.

Aspects of Scientific Explanation, Collier, 1965.

Hospers, J. *An Introduction to Philosophical Analysis,* Routledge, 1956.

Hume, D. *A Treatise of Human Nature,* 1739; ed. L. A. Selby-Bigge, OUP, 1888.

Enquiries, 1748, 1752; ed. L. A. Selby-Bigge, OUP, 1902.

Juhos, B. 'Empiricism and Physicalism', *Analysis* (1935).

Kant, I. *Critique of Pure Reason,* 1781.

Groundwork of the Metaphysic of Morals, 1785.

Critique of Practical Reason, 1788.

Kneale, M. and W. C. *The development of Logic,* OUP, 1962.

Kraft, V. *The Vienna Circle,* Greenwood, 1953.

Kripke, S. 'Naming and Necessity' in G. Harman and D. Davidson (eds.) *Semantics of Natural Language,* Reidel, 1973.

Kuhn, T. *The Structure of Scientific Revolutions,* Univ. of Chicago Press, 1962.

Lazerowitz, M. 'The Principle of Verifiability', in *Mind* (1937).

The Structure of Metaphysics, Routledge, 1955.

Leibniz, G. W. *Philosophical Writings,* ed. G. H. R. Parkinson, Dent, 1973.

Locke, John *An Essay Concerning Human Understanding,* 1690.

Luckhardt, C. G. (ed.) *Wittgenstein: Sources and Perspectives,* Cornell UP, 1979.

Lyas, C. (ed.) *Philosophy and Linguistics,* Macmillan, 1971.

Macdonald, G. F. (ed.) *Perception and Identity,* Macmillan, 1979.

Magee, B. (ed.) *Men of Ideas,* BBC, 1978.

Malcolm, N. *Knowledge and Certainty,* Prentice Hall, 1963.

Mill, J. S. *Utilitarianism*, 1863.
    A System of Logic, 1843.
    An Examination of Sir William Hamilton's Philosophy, 1865.
Moore, G. E. *Philosophical Papers*, Allen & Unwin, 1959.
    Principia Ethica, CUP, 1903.
    Ethics, HUL, 1912; 2nd edn., OUP, 1966.
Neurath, O. 'Wissenschaftliche Weltauffassung — Der Wiener Kreis' (with Rudolf Carnap and Hans Hahn), in *Erkenntnis* I. A translation appears in M. Neurath and R. S. Cohen (eds.), *Otto Neurath: Empiricism and Sociology*, Reidel, 1973.
Neurath, O., Carnap, R. and Morris, C. (eds.), *Foundations of the Unity of Science*, volumes I and II, University of Chicago Press, 1969. Originally published as *International Encyclopedia of Unified Science*, ed. O. Neurath et al., University of Chicago Press, 1938.
O'Connor, D. J. 'Some Consequences of Professor Ayer's Verification Principle' in *Analysis* (1949–50).
Passmore, J. A. 'Logical Positivism' (in three parts), in *Australasian Journal of Psychology and Philosophy* (1943, 1944 and 1948).
Popper, K. R. *The Logic of Scientific Discovery*, Hutchinson, 1959.
Reichenbach, H. *The Rise of Scientific Philosophy*, Univ. of California, 1951.
Russell, B. *Introduction to Mathematical Philosophy*, Allen & Unwin, 1919.
    Logic and Knowledge, ed. R. C. Marsh, Allen & Unwin, 1956.
    'The Philosophy of Logical Atomism' in D. Pears (ed.) *Russell's Logical Atomism*, Fontana, 1972.
Russell, L. J. 'Communication and Verification' in *Proceedings of the Aristotelian Society*, supp. vol. (1934).
Ryle, G. *Dilemmas*, CUP, 1966.
Rynin, D. 'Vindication of L*G*C*L P*S*T*V*SM' in *Proceedings and Addresses of the American Philosophical Association* (1957).
Schleichert, H. (ed.) *Logischer Empirismus – der Wiener Kreis*, Wilhelm Fink, 1975.
Schlick, M. *Problems of Ethics*, 1939; Dover, 1962.
    Gesammelte Aufsätze Georg Olms, 1969.
    Philosophical Papers, vol. II (1925–36), Reidel, 1979.
Stevenson, C. L. *Ethics and Language*, Yale, 1944.
    Facts and Values, Yale, 1963.
Strawson, P. F. *The Bounds of Sense*, Methuen, 1966.
Thakur, S. C. *Philosophy and Psychical Research*, Allen & Unwin, 1976.
Urmson, J. O. *Philosophical Analysis*, OUP 1967.
    The Emotive Theory of Ethics, Hutchinson, 1968.
Vesey, G. *Perception*, Doubleday, 1971.

Waismann, F. *The Principles of Linguistic Philosophy,* Macmillan, 1965.
  Ludwig Wittgenstein und der Wiener Kreis, Blackwell, 1967. (Trans.
  as *Ludwig Wittgenstein and the Vienna Circle,* Blackwell, 1979.)
  How I see Philosophy, Macmillan, 1968.
White, A. R. *Truth,* Macmillan, 1970.
Wisdom, J. O. 'Metamorphoses of the Verifiability Theory of Meaning'
  in *Mind* (1963).
Wittgenstein, L. *Tractatus Logico-Philosophicus,* 1921; trans. D. F.
  Pears and B. F. McGuinness, Routledge, 1961.
  Philosophical Investigations, Blackwell, 1958.
  The Blue and Brown Books, Blackwell, 1964.
  Philosophische Bemerkungen, Blackwell, 1964. (Trans. as *Philoso-
  phical Remarks,* Blackwell, 1975.)
  'Lecture on Ethics', in *Philosophical Review* (1965).
  Zettel, Blackwell, 1967.

INDEX

WITHDRAWN
FROM
COLLECTION

FORDHAM
UNIVERSITY
LIBRARIES